A Wife's PRAYER

Seeking god's best for your husband

PAMELA HINES

WHITAKER
HOUSE

A WIFE'S PRAYER:
Seeking God's Best for Your Husband

Pamela Hines
P.O. Box 241040
Milwaukee, WI 53224
www.hinesfeet.com

ISBN: 978-0-88368-204-3
Printed in the United States of America
© 2007 by Pamela Hines

1030 Hunt Valley Circle
New Kensington, PA 15068
www.whitakerhouse.com

Library of Congress Cataloging-in Publication Data
Hines, Pamela, 1961–
A wife's prayer : seeking God's best for your husband / Pamela Hines.
p. cm.
Summary: "By providing Scriptures and examples of prayers, which are grouped together under a wide range of topics, the author encourages women to intercede for their husbands"—Provided by publisher.
ISBN 978-0-88368-204-3 (trade pbk. : alk. paper) 1. Wives—Prayers and devotions. 2. Christian women—Prayers and devotions. I. Title.
BV4844.H56 2007
242'.8435—dc22   2007012418

1 2 3 4 5 6 7 8 9 10 11 12 ᴜᴜ 15 14 13 12 11 10 09 08 07

DEDICATION

hroughout the years, many women in some way influenced my life and it would take several pages to appreciate them all. God has blessed me to walk with and touch some of His greatest. I greatly admire the faithfulness of God, toward me through women.

There are, however, four women whom I can truly say contributed in a variety of ways to who I am today as a woman, wife, mother, and minister, and I dedicate this book to their impartations and godly examples.

*To my belated **Hazel Westmoreland,** my mother, the most phenomenal representation of a woman I have ever known. She laid the foundation and prepared my life for every truth of womanhood that would ever come my way. Through her own life and experiences, I learned submission; through her acts of unconditional love, I learned the key to success in any relationship. Although my mother is with the Lord, her legacy lives on, and my desire is to be half the woman my mother was. I love and miss you, mom.*

*To my precious mother-in-law, **Corener Hines,** I cannot take total credit for this project. It was your* *sensitivity to the voice of the Holy Spirit when He said, "Marriages are under attack," that I was led to my knees. Thank you for sharing what you heard in prayer. You have always been a powerful example of a praying wife and mother. I have learned so many things sitting at your feet and watching as you walk with God. Since the age of twelve, you have been a mother, mentor, confidant, and friend. I owe much of who I am today to you. I love you deeply. Thank you for birthing and giving me (apart from Jesus Christ) the best gift of all, my husband, Bishop Darrell L. Hines.*

*To **Bishop Earnestine Cleveland Reems-Dickerson**, who gave me the courage to stand in ministry with my husband. You have been an inspiration to women all over the world as well as me. I am proud to call you my spiritual mom and friend. Thank you for your love and support through the years.*

*To **Mother Smith**, who gave me my first book on being a wife. I learned and experienced a lot since that book, but will always be grateful for the seed you sowed into my life.*

CONTENTS

FOREWORD

J married Pam over twenty-five years ago. When I married her, I had no idea that she was going to be such a tremendous woman of God. Pam has always been a beautiful person, but what she has become as a mature woman of God is something wonderful to behold. She is truly an anointed vessel of God, chosen for such a time as this.

My wife has always had a prayer life, but I had no idea of the intensity of the prayers she prayed. She denies herself and immerses into God as she prays continually. She prays concerning my life as her husband, as a pastor, and as a man of God.

When I first read this book, I did not know what to expect. But the opening paragraphs quickly revealed that I was in for a life-changing experience. As a husband, it is so encouraging to know that my wife prays with such detail and fervor concerning my life. I encourage every woman to read this book in faith, believing that God does answer prayer. I would not be the man of God I am today had my wife not travailed with faith-filled prayers. I am living proof of the power of *A Wife's Prayer*.

—*Darrell L. Hines*

INTRODUCTION

*A*s wives, we often pray *about* our husbands instead of *for* our husbands. And, we do so with incorrect motives. Beyond all of our good and pure intensions there is a strong desire to go before the throne of God and "tell on him." We want our husbands to act the way we want them to act, instead of the way God wants them to act. If you are anything like me, you have surely discovered this type of prayer does not work because it is self-seeking.

The Word of God declares that our prayers avail much. (See James 5:16.) Our prayers are dynamic in their working; they are powerful and effective. If we believe what we pray, our prayers will move mountains. (See Mark 11:23.) However, if you do not see results, you may need to modify the content of your prayers as well as the manner in which you are praying. Remember, the desired result is to see your husband walking according to the will of God, not according to your will. When he walks as God desires, change is inevitable.

As new covenant believers, we need to pray the answer instead of complaining about the sins and shortcomings of our husbands. The Word of God should be the focus of our prayers. God responds to His Word, not to our crying and complaining. When we pray and approach things from His Word, we open the door for God's desires to manifest.

11

Through the prayers within this book, my desire is simply to declare before God the promises that He has spoken concerning our husbands. In Job 22:28, God says, *"Thou shalt also decree a thing, and it shall be established unto thee"* (KJV). Therefore, as we pray for our husbands, we will declare His truth and promises in our husbands' lives, whether or not we currently see them in the natural.

Even if your husband is not walking with God, praying based upon the Word is a sure way to build your faith and see results. Make no mistake about it; your husband can walk completely submitted to God. Jesus fully paid the price for your husband to walk with God. He already sees your husband saved, healed, prosperous, and delivered. Now it is up to you to purpose in your heart to see him in the same manner.

I am not encouraging you to ignore what you may be experiencing with your husband. However, praying based upon the Word of God will place you above your circumstances instead of beneath the weight of them.

It is my desire that you will pray uninhibitedly concerning your husband. If you need to repent for holding a grudge or harboring unforgiveness, release it and let it go. While you are praying, this will give you the freedom to focus on what God has spoken in His Word—and nothing else.

I have personally prayed for your husband, along with every woman who may ever touch this book. Never forget that those things we are petitioning God for, through Jesus Christ, are already in our husbands. We are simply praying them into manifestation. Your desire for love and respect is already in him; walking with God is in him; providing for your family is in him. If he is a Christian, everything your husband will ever need in order to be the man that he is destined to be is already residing in him, in Christ. If he is not a Christian, stand strong in the confession of your faith and continue living your life in a manner that will draw him to Christ. *"That even if some* [husbands] *do not obey the word, they, without a word, may be won by the conduct of their wives"* (1 Peter 3:1).

As you pray these prayers, wherever you see the words "my husband," replace them with your husband's name. It will make the prayers meaningful, as well as more personal. I want to encourage you to pray deliberately; pour your heart out for your husband and sow this prayer seed into his life.

As you pray, you will see God tenderly bring change in your husband's life. At the same time, He will also begin to fill your life with His presence.

As you pray for your husband, and see the miracles that God can do, it is my hope that you might grow in your understanding of how powerful and dynamic prayer can be. Perhaps you will become a mighty prayer warrior who faithfully interceeds for your family, friends, church, and city. *"The effective, fervent prayer of a righteous* [woman] *avails much"* (James 5:16).

God Bless You,

—*Pamela Hines*

MY STORY OF EFFECTIVE PRAYER

I met my husband in 1971 at the age of twelve—it really was love at first sight. Although he was three years my senior, I knew he would be the love of my life. A month after graduating from high school, before a bridal party of forty-three individuals, I became Mrs. Darrell L. Hines.

Life as a young bride was quite challenging. Although I knew my husband came from a Christian home, I did not know that the most influential individuals in his life were his uncles. He learned many things from his uncles—some good; some not so good. One of the "not so good" lessons learned was his understanding of the role of women, particularly that of a wife.

My husband loved me and was a wonderful provider, something he learned from his own father. He always worked as I stayed home to care for our home and children. But my husband also believed that women had little to no say at all in the marriage; he believed that a woman's place was in the home and that she should be at the disposal of her husband's every desire. Not knowing any better as a young bride, I submitted myself totally to these demands. Eventually, after many years of unreasonable demands, I needed change.

Many things transpired within the first seven years of our marriage, but one would prove to be a major turning point in our lives. On July 17, 1981, I was scheduled to fly to Memphis, Tennessee, to visit my relatives. While seated on the plane, I prayed a simple prayer, "Lord, don't let my husband cheat on me." That was it.

When my husband went to lunch that day, he decided to stop at one of the airport restaurants to grab a bite to eat. While there, a woman propositioned him, and he agreed to meet her after concluding his evening shift at work. At that time, my husband was a member of an airport grounds crew, often assisting in positioning aircrafts to their assigned station. On this particular night, a thunderstorm gathered as he helped with the routine arrival of a DC-9 from Chicago. He guided the plane to its station and positioned the plane's stairway. As he began his assent up the stairs to the door, a bolt of lightening struck the tail of the aircraft. When my husband grabbed the rail of the aircraft door, he was thrown forty-five feet into the air. His heart immediately stopped as coworkers attempted to administer CPR. When the paramedics arrived on the scene, my husband showed no vital signs. In fact, the medical records from St. Luke's Medical Center state that: "The patient fell to the ground. Nearby observers started CPR. Paramedics found patient...without pulse, respiration, or blood pressure."

An airline supervisor, a God-fearing Baptist woman who rode in the ambulance with my husband, said that he had no heartbeat for forty-five minutes. She also stated that the Spirit of the Lord came into the ambulance in a palpable way. When it did, she could sense that a miracle might be in the working. However, when she touched his hand, it was as cold as ice. She immediately began to pray for my husband. As she did, the EKG suddenly picked up a reading; God gave my husband back his life.

When they arrived at the hospital, doctors said my husband was screaming, moaning, and his body convulsing as he yelled out "Lord, bless my soul. Save me, Jesus!" continuously. As reported by the *Milwaukee Sentinel*, more than eighty people showed up to pray at the hospital. The number of visitors was so unusual, hospital workers thought he was some kind of celebrity. In spite of the overwhelming support and prayers, my husband's situation looked bleak. Doctors determined that he would not live through the night and, if he did, he would have permanent brain damage. However, the doctors did not know that God had a plan for my husband's life. Before long, the persistence of those praying paid off. My husband's screams turned to a repeated supplication, "Lord, bless my soul." For hours, he repeatedly cried out for God to bless his soul until he eventually fell asleep.

The next morning, as I stood over my husband, he awoke with amnesia. I told him that I was his wife and I was carrying his child, but he did not recognize or believe me. I raised my shirt to show him my very pregnant stomach but his words were, "I didn't do that!" And he fell asleep.

I began to pray, saying, "Lord, when he wakes up, I want him to know me. He does not have to know his mother, his father, his sisters, or his brother, but he has to know me." And I was done. When my husband awoke again, he opened his eyes, smiled, and said, "Hi honey." I praised God

for answering my prayer. As time moved on, my husband's health was restored, and today he has a worldwide ministry.

One little prayer, "Lord, don't let my husband cheat on me," and the course of our lives was changed forever. God did not cause my husband to be struck by lightning. I believe it was my husband's decision to join that woman in the restaurant that opened the door to the enemy in his life.

Prayer is a very powerful tool. Through the avenue of prayer, we can move mountains, change circumstances, and connect with the purpose of God in the earth.

Over the years, I cried because I wanted change in my husband's life, but nothing happened until I began to pray. Not prayers of complaint and discouragement, but prayers based upon the Word of God. That is when change happened. Many times, it seemed as though things were getting worse. Nevertheless, I stayed with it, and I did not back down. I fully believe in the power of prayer. It has manifested itself in my life and marriage. It can do the same for you.

How A Wife's Prayer Started

*I*n April of 2003, after counseling scores of women who were experiencing troubled or failed marriages, I sought the Lord to reveal ways that would help the marriages within our church as well as those within the body of Christ. For so long, Christians have exercised their faith to believe for cars and homes but failed to use that same faith to believe for whole, healthy marriage relationships.

After waiting quietly and patiently before God, He revealed His answer. In May of that year, I announced to our congregation that we would be hosting a time of prayer where married women could come and lay the burdens, joys, cares, and concerns about their husbands on the altar before God.

The time of prayer took place at 5:00 a.m. on a Saturday morning, and the agenda was heartfelt, focused prayer. Expecting only a handful of female prayer warriors, I was surprised to find hundreds of women awaiting my arrival; some arriving by cabs and buses as early as 4:00 a.m. As I entered the sanctuary that morning, I knew that God not only ordained this, but He also marked it as a time for an encounter with Him that would affect our lives forever.

As we began, I gave the women the same instructions that God had given me. We were going to pray, but we were only going to pray the Word of God. We were not going to pray our own agendas and desires. We were going to pray the answer, not the problem. And that is what we did.

What transpired during that time of prayer is something that I will never forget. As we began to pray, I could sense the anointing. As we moved forward, I knew yokes and burdens were being destroyed. The presence of God was profound that morning, and a great sense of joy and accomplishment rested upon each of us when we departed. This book is based upon the prayers we spoke that day. It is my prayer that they will continue to change and transform lives around the world as they did for those who prayed that day.

Here are just a few testimonies of women who prayed that morning.

TESTIMONY: When Pastor Pamela announced that we would be praying for our husbands, I was a little apprehensive. I felt like I needed prayer more than my husband did. But out of obedience, and because I loved to pray, I joined her and the other women. At the time, my husband had an ongoing battle with unforgiveness, which I allowed to affect every area of our life. Our finances, our health, and our marriage itself were in trouble. I was angry because I knew that walking in the love of God was essential to the blessings of God. In my mind, his failure to walk in love was drying up our finances and my anger towards him was making me physically sick. We both were to blame.

Because he was angry, my husband became numb to spiritual things and slowly began to decline in his walk with God. I did the same because I had become very judgmental and angry. In my heart, I wanted an answer but could not seem to settle down long enough to get one.

When I attended the prayer service, I began to repeat after Pastor Pamela, but initially, not with my whole heart. Repeatedly she spoke the Word of God as she prayed for husbands. I could feel the love of God overwhelming me. I began to pray earnestly for my husband out of the flow of love moving within me. I did so until I sensed a breakthrough. This powerful experience saved my marriage. After the prayer service ended, I cried all the way home and walked up to my husband and apologized for every negative word that I had spoken to him. I apologized for not listening to him and for judging him. For months, every time I thought about that experience in prayer, I cried. Then I realized that as I sowed the seed of prayer for my husband, God changed me. Today, my husband lives free of bitterness and strife. He is committed to God and His Word. Additionally, our marriage is healthy and strong.

—M. Henderson

TESTIMONY: Prior to my husband accepting Jesus Christ, he was addicted to drugs. When his best friend came to the Lord, he then shared Jesus Christ with my husband. As soon as my husband

heard the Word of God, he abandoned the drugs and ran whole-heartedly to follow Christ. Four years after accepting Christ, he was working full-time in ministry.

After his father died and several other trials, he found himself slowly beginning a downward spiral into a backslidden state. It was not long after that he began using drugs again. Abandoning our home for several days at a time, money disappearing, irrational behavior, losing the desire to attend church—all the attributes of his addiction were now in full bloom in our life.

I was carrying our first child, and my husband's absence brought great stress to me as well as our marriage. He was gone for two years. I only heard his voice on the answering machine. Sometimes the phone would ring with him on the other end, saying nothing. I spent many nights in solitude, crying and praying that God would deliver my husband. I believed in the power of prayer and in God's ability to change my situation, but those two years were the worst years of my life. There were times I was overwhelmed, not knowing where he was or if he was okay. I never wanted out of my marriage; I did, however, want the situation to end.

When Pastor Pamela announced we would be praying for our husbands, I knew I needed to be there because I was at the end of my rope. I needed God to bring total deliverance to my husband. I was among the

first of the women to arrive that morning. There was great expectancy in the atmosphere. As we prayed, my heart softened as Pastor Pamela read the Word of God over our husband's lives. Prostrate on the floor, I cried out to God for my husband until, in my heart, I could sense a breaking in his life. As our time of prayer came to an end, Pastor Pamela began to speak under the inspiration of the Holy Spirit. She called my name and told me that the Lord said, "Stop crying and do not tell another soul what you are going through." Through Pastor Pamela, the Lord went on to say, "I have your husband in My hand, and I'm calling him back to the straight and narrow, and I will restore him. You often ask, 'Where is the respect?' But your husband admires you more than you know. Your husband's situation has run its course, and after this time of prayer, his life will never be the same again." This was the confirmation I needed, so I began to rejoice for what God had done.

Immediately after that day, I began to notice changes in my husband's situation. The first changes were his return home, his desire to repent (getting his heart right with God), and his desire to attend church again. Slowly and methodically, I could see the hand of God working on my husband. His hunger for the Word of God began to manifest again, as well as his desire to fulfill God's call on his life. Today, my husband is committed to Christ, teaching the Word of God, helping to restore others who are in a backslidden state. I thank God for the power of

prayer and for Pastor Pamela's willingness to obey God. —Levon Berry

TESTIMONY: I am the wife of an unsaved husband. For many years, my husband had cheated, lied, neglected our children, and threatened to leave the marriage. I was desperate to hear from God. I did not want to lose my husband, but something had to change, or we were not going to make it.

I had never heard of women gathering to pray for their husbands. As I listened to your prayer, I began to weep because of the things you were saying. I could sense God's presence. After several days, the atmosphere in my house changed. My husband was used to coming home to a fight, but instead came home to a clean, peaceful home. Our marriage is still in great need of God's touch, but I can see changes, mostly in me. The arguing has almost stopped and my husband is spending more time with our children.

—Andrea C.

It is my prayer that you will experience the same transforming power that we witnessed on that morning in May of 2003. And why shouldn't you? We have the same God, yesterday, today, and tomorrow. (See Hebrews 13:8.) Expect your life to change; expect God to overshadow your husband as you pray for him in faith.

God bless you; my prayers are with you.

Chapter 1

A WIFE'S PRAYER FOR HERSELF

*Before you pray, I want you to prepare your heart.
Praying with the right heart is an essential
element to powerful prayer.*

Heavenly Father, in the name of Jesus, Your Word instructs me to enter into Your gates with thanksgiving and into Your courts with praise. Therefore I thank and praise You for being my Father. I recognize and acknowledge this is the day that You have made, and I rejoice and am glad in it. I praise You for giving me the heart to pray out Your will for my husband.

Thank You for loving me and for being a Savior who is fully aware of my weaknesses, as well as those of my husband. Thank You that I am strong in You and in the power of Your might. I praise You that I can boldly approach Your throne of grace, receiving the strength, ability, and wisdom necessary to be a godly wife and to pray out Your plan for my husband's life.

Give me the grace I need today so I can accomplish all that is set before me. You told me that if I were to acknowledge You in all of my ways, You would direct and make clear my path. Therefore, I acknowledge You and give You place so I can receive all that is necessary for this day. Your Word is a lamp unto my feet and light unto my path.

Thank You for Your mercies, which are new every morning, and I can draw on those mercies when and if I make a mistake. Thank You for loving me with an unconditional love and for pouring that love into my heart, helping me love my husband, children, and those whom You have placed within my life.

I thank You, Father, that I will be subject (submitted and adapted) to my husband in everything just as the church is subject to Christ according to Ephesians 5:24 (AMP). Give me strength to cast down my thoughts so they can come in line with the Word of God and the obedience of Christ. Concerning my husband, I want to think about him the way You think. I will respect him as You have instructed me, which means that I will notice him, regard him, honor him, prefer him, venerate him, esteem him, praise him, love him, and admire him.

With all that I have to do, I trust in You and I know You will move mountains on my behalf. I take this time today and every day to reach for You so that my husband will reach for You. Thank You that it is so.

In Jesus' name, Amen.

Chapter 2

MY HUSBAND'S DESIRES

In our society, it is the norm to see images of immorality and idolatry fighting for our husbands' attention. Internet pornography, secular television, even some popular women's magazines are designed to feed their physical senses and appetites. Unless they intentionally choose to ignore the pull of the world, many husbands are lured into yielding to evil desires. We can never forget what Jesus said in Luke 22:46, "Pray, lest you enter into temptation." Know that the temptations that they face will not overcome them when we faithfully and consistently surround them with a spirit of prayer.

Father, I thank and praise You that my husband's desires are based on Your Word; they are pure in Your sight. You are my husband's delight. May his love for You take priority over any and every thing in his life. I pray he will delight himself in You; grant him the desires of his heart. Make his desires righteous and grant them according to Your Word.

Mark 4:19; Psalm 119:16, 37:40

ather, because my husband fears You, fulfill the desires of his heart and answer his cry. Thank You that as You fulfill the desires of his heart, Your whole purpose will manifest in his life.

Psalm 145:19, 20:4

hatever my husband petitions You for, strengthen his heart so he believes and therefore receives, for You said he would have whatever he says. I thank You that You will not deny the requests spoken from my husband's lips. Give him the confidence to know that when he asks anything according to Your will, You do hear him.

1 John 5:14; Mark 11:23–25

n times past, my husband lived his life fulfilling the desires of his flesh and of his mind, but today is a new day. I pray he will no longer live his life feeding the appetites of his flesh. Deliver him from the lust of his flesh, obsessions, and any form of laziness. Help him to remove impure thoughts or immorality.

Give him the strength and knowledge he needs to keep sin from reigning in his mortal body or fulfilling its desires. Keep his desires pure and righteous so he may always live in Your presence. I declare my husband takes delight in You and Your Word. You shall fulfill the desires of his heart.

Romans 6:12; Ephesians 2:3; Psalm 37:4

ather, Your Word says that what the righteous desires will be given to him. Thank You for giving my husband the desires of his heart when they line up with Your

Word. Never allow my husband to isolate himself or have self-ish desires. Do not let him rebel against sound judgment.

Proverbs 10:24, 18:1

ather, bless my husband with wealth and honor, that he may not lack in what he desires for himself. I pray my husband keeps his heart right in You so when Your Word enters his heart, it will produce godly results in his life. I pray he guards his heart from the worries of this age, the deceit-fulness of wealth, and the desire for other things. I declare these things will not enter in and choke the Word making it unfruitful in his life, because You've kept his heart.

Ecclesiastes 6:2; Matthew 13:22

pray my husband will put on the Lord Jesus Christ and make no plans to satisfy fleshly desires. Father, give him knowledge to crucify the flesh with its passions and desires. Thank You that my husband lives as one who has taken off his former way of life, that old man corrupted by deceitful desires, and is living the life of a newly created indi-vidual.

Romans 13:14; Galatians 5:24; Ephesians 4:22

ather I declare my husband walks in a way that does not fulfill lustful desires, a way that is unlike those who do not know You. Keep his life pure before You. Do not allow him to be enticed by his own evil desires. Help him to crucify the works of his flesh and cast down sinful thoughts in his mind.

1 Thessalonians 4:5; James 1:14

I pray my husband refuses to ask You for things he would use to consume his own lust. Instead, I pray his prayers are those consistent with the Word. As an obedient servant, my husband will not be conformed to the desires of his former ignorance, but he will live out his remaining days on this earth focused on Your will.

James 4:3; 1 Peter 1:14, 4:2

L ord, I thank You that daily my husband desires Your Word, the living water, as his gift from You.

Revelation 22:17

Chapter 3

MY HUSBAND'S STRENGTH

*For many years, my husband endeavored to live his
life governed by his own strength. After much toil, he
soon found his strength had limitations. By submitting
himself to the Word of God, he began to see that
God's strength is limitless. When my husband finally
abandoned his own way of doing things, he stepped
out of his own strength, which symbolized his way of
doing things, and stepped over into God's way of doing
things. Victory has accompanied his life since making
that decision.*

Father, I pray that my husband is strong and courageous in You and in the power of Your might. I
pray he is on guard and stands firm in what he believes. I
pray that my husband keeps Your Word continually before
him, that he is watchful and not ignorant of Satan's wicked
devices.

Ephesians 6:10; 1 Corinthians 16:13; 2 Corinthians 2:11

I pray my husband waits upon You and when he does, You strengthen his heart. Thank You that he recognizes You as his salvation and light, the strength of his life leaving no place in him for fear. You, Lord, are my husband's rock, his fortress, and his deliverer. You are his God and his strength; it is in You he will trust. You are his buckler and the horn of his salvation; You are his high tower.

Psalm 27:1, 18:2

I pray my husband finds the joy of the Lord as his strength. That when he feels weak he will boldly declare and acknowledge that You are the strength of his life. Let Your grace manifest sufficiently for him and Your strength be made perfect in his times of weakness.

Joel 3:10; 2 Corinthians 12:9

T hank You, Father, that, as my husband waits upon You, his strength is renewed in You. Let him mount up on wings as an eagle, run and not be weary, allowing him to walk and not faint. Do not allow him to stagger at Your promise, but to be strong in faith, giving glory to You.

Isaiah 40:31

F ather, I pray my husband stands strong in the grace of our Lord and Savior, Jesus Christ. I ask You to stand with my husband and strengthen him that Your Word will be fully known in his life. For You are his strength; You are his song and his salvation.

2 Timothy 2:1; Exodus 15:2

My Husband's *Strength*

*L*ord, I thank You that my husband loves You with all his heart, with all his soul, and with all his strength. I pray he keeps every command You have given so he may have the strength to cross into and possess the land You have promised him.

Deuteronomy 6:5, 11:8

*G*ive him the strength he needs for as long as he lives. Keep things in perspective for my husband. Do not allow him to forget that riches and honor come from You. You are the ruler of everything. In Your hand are power and might, and it is in Your hand to make a man great and to give strength to all. Help him seek Your face always, never the face of riches and prestige.

1 Chronicles 29:12, 16:11

I thank You, Father, that when my husband grieves, he will remember his strength comes from rejoicing in You. He will know that wisdom, understanding, comfort, and counsel all belong to You.

Nehemiah 8:10

*F*ather, thank You for clothing my husband with strength and for making his way perfect. You are his shield, and he can trust in You. Thank You for being his refuge and a very pleasant help in times of trouble.

Psalm 18:32, 46:1, 28:7

*F*ather, I pray my husband sees his obligation to bear the weaknesses of those without strength, and not to please himself. I pray he knows God's foolishness is wiser

 A *Wife's* **Prayer**

than human wisdom, and God's weakness is stronger than human strength.

Romans 15:1; 1 Corinthians 1:25

*L*ord, let my husband's company be those who love You. Allow him to surround himself with men who are strong and courageous in You.

Isaiah 41:6

I pray my husband labors and strives with Your strength, because it works powerfully in him. When he speaks, allow his speech to be like the oracles of God. When he serves, let his service be from the strength You provide so that in everything glory comes to You, through Jesus Christ. To You belong the glory and the power forever and ever.

Colossians 1:29; 1 Peter 4:11

Chapter 4

MY HUSBAND'S REST

*One of the greatest challenges for me within my
marriage is getting my husband to settle down long
enough to rest. The demands of ministry are nonstop
and because he is known nationwide and in many
countries around the world, the pull on his life is
tremendous. God never intended for His servants
to work themselves to death. Hebrews clearly states,
"There remains therefore a rest for the people of
God" (Hebrews 4:9). As our greatest example, Jesus
often took time away from the people and the work of
ministry in order to rest. Through prayer, we can
help our husbands walk in the wisdom of God and
receive the necessary rest so they can fulfill
the will of God for their lives.*

Father, I pray my husband walks in wisdom and, as he
comes to You, that You give him rest. I pray he takes
Your yoke upon him so that he learns of You. You are meek and
lowly in heart. Give him rest for his soul for Your yoke is easy

and Your burden is light. Your presence brings refreshment and rest. I declare my husband understands the importance of relaxation.

Matthew 11:28–30; Exodus 33:14

*L*ord, I pray my husband slows down and sanctifies one day of the week that belongs to You. Keep work far from him on that day and allow him to be refreshed in Your presence.

Deuteronomy 5:14; Leviticus 23:32

I pray my husband finds himself among those who believe and, because they do, they enter into the rest that remains for the people of God. May he cease from his own works and labors to enter into Your rest. Keep patterns of disobedience away from my husband so that he can live in Your place of rest.

Hebrews 4:9–11

*F*ather, let my husband not be anxious but patiently wait on You, for You cause the weary to find their place of rest.

Philippians 4:6; Isaiah 28:12

I pray my husband will follow the example of Jesus who called His disciples to a resting place. Give him the wisdom to take a vacation and retreat from his work in order to rest his soul and his body. Thank You for teaching him how to be renewed.

Mark 6:31; 2 Corinthians 4:16

*F*ather, when my husband is feeling overwhelmed, give him the wisdom to go away by himself to a remote place and rest a little.

Mark 6:31

*F*ather, I thank You that my husband lies down in peace; only You make him dwell in safety. I pray my husband will walk in complete and absolute trust in You and never be afraid. When he lies down, his sleep will be sound and sweet.

Psalm 4:8

Chapter 5

MY HUSBAND'S HEALTH

In 2004, my husband began to notice a series of physical changes in his body, many of which were diet related. It has been said that nearly 80 percent of all illnesses are related to the way we eat. After receiving negative reports concerning his health from his physician, my husband decided to change his diet. Within weeks he lost weight, had a resurgence of energy, and improved his overall health. God wants our husbands to experience divine health, not just divine healing. Your prayers will keep your husband's heart sensitive to God's voice concerning his physical well-being.

Father, I pray my husband finds physical healing in Your Word because You are Jehovah Rapha, my husband's physician, the Lord who heals him. Keep him in good physical health.

Exodus 15:26

I pray my husband acknowledges Your benefits daily and never forgets, for You are the One who forgives his iniquities. You heal all of his diseases before he ever cries unto You. Thank You for healing him.

Psalm 30:2, 103:2–3

*T*hank You for sending the Word to heal and deliver my husband from any destruction. You were wounded for his transgressions and You were bruised for his iniquities. The chastisement of his peace was upon You, and by Your stripes my husband is healed.

Isaiah 53:5; 1 Peter 2:24

*T*hank You for bearing my husband's sins in Your own body. He is now dead to sin, sickness, and disease because of Your redemptive work. I pray, when my husband hears the Word concerning healing, that he receives You and healing manifests in his body. Thank You for taking sickness away from my husband's presence.

Exodus 23:25; Luke 9:11; Galatians 2:20

*F*ather, Your Word declares that You have redeemed my husband from the curse of the law and from sickness. You have given him health. For poverty, You have given my husband wealth; for death, You have given him abundant life. Thank You that the curse of sickness is broken over my husband.

Galatians 3:13

I declare my husband prospers and lives in health just as his soul prospers and lives in health. I pray he pays close attention to Your words and incline his ears to Your sayings. Let not Your Word depart from his eyes. Give him the strength to keep Your words in the middle of his heart because Your words are life and healing to all of his flesh.

Proverbs 4:20–22; 3 John 1:2

I thank You, Father, that my husband will not forget Your law. He will keep Your commandments and, in so doing, length of days, long life, and peace will be added to him.

Proverbs 3:1–2

*F*ather, thank You that my husband does not consider himself to be wise, but he fears You and turns away from evil. Therefore, it will be healing for his body and strengthening for his bones. May the Son of Righteousness rise with healing in His wings so that he can go out and playfully jump like "stall-fed calves."

Malachi 4:2; Psalm 3:7–8

*L*ord, I pray my husband be not as one who speaks rashly, or one whose tongue is like a piercing sword; but may he have a tongue of the wise that brings healing to his life as well as the lives of others.

Proverbs 12:18

I pray my husband will eat the way You have instructed him so that he will prosper in his physical body. I pray he eat his fill of foods that You have made to increase and prosper his physical well-being.

Deuteronomy 12:25, 31:20

Chapter 6

MY HUSBAND'S AFFECTIONS

Many women discover that their husbands have placed their affections in other things or in other people. God gave your husband the emotion of affection; however, the lust of the flesh, the pride of life, and the lust of the eyes will tempt him to place those affections in the wrong place. Through prayer, we can build a hedge of protection around our husbands' affections so that they can be channeled toward God. When channeled toward God, He will ensure that your husband's affections are redirected toward you and your family. But prayer is essential.

Father, I pray that my husband's passions are toward You first, then toward me and our family. I pray he prioritizes what is most important in Your eyes. Make him zealously affectionate in good and righteous things. Let his affections increase toward You as he dwells in Your house, like Your servant David, and his inward affections would be toward helping the people of God.

Psalm 61:4; Galatians 4:18

*T*hank You that my husband is raised with Christ. I pray he set his affections on things that are above, and not on the things of this world. Open his eyes that he may see that he is not limited by man, but by his own affections if they are not in line with Your Word.

Colossians 3:2; 2 Corinthians 6:12

*L*ord, I pray my husband shows brotherly affection toward others and outdoes others in showing them love and honor. I thank You that others will pray for him and show him great affection because of Your grace upon his life.

Romans 12:10; 2 Corinthians 9:14

*F*ather, I pray my husband will make every effort to supplement his faith with goodness, goodness with knowledge, knowledge with self-control, self-control with endurance, endurance with godliness, godliness with brotherly affection, and brotherly affection with love. If these qualities are his and are increasing, they will keep him from being useless or unfruitful in the knowledge of our Lord Jesus Christ. Do not let him be the person who lacks these things, walking blind and shortsighted like one who has forgotten he is cleansed of his past sins.

2 Corinthians 1:5–9

Chapter 7

MY HUSBAND'S PROSPERITY

*For years, my husband and I struggled financially.
After living on welfare for many years, and struggling
to have our basic needs met, we decided to begin
operating in the principles of the kingdom of God.
After many days and nights of praying, God began to
reveal to us, through His Word and other men and
women of God, that His desire was for us to prosper
in every area of our lives, including financially. When
you prosper financially, you are enabled to become a
blessing to someone else. More than twenty years ago,
God told my husband, "If you take care of My business,
I will take care of you." God kept His word, and
continues to keep it to this day.*

Father, the world has the idea that prosperity is simply financial blessing, but I pray my husband recognizes that real prosperity is not possible without You. I thank You that my husband's abundance is in You; he prospers and operates in good health as his soul prospers.

3 John 1:2

I pray my husband obeys and serves You. I pray he will spend his days in prosperity and his years in Your presence. Let him meditate on Your Word and make his way prosperous, so that he has good success and whatever he does prospers.

Job 36:11; Joshua 1:8; Nehemiah 2:20

*T*hank You, Lord, that as my husband seeks You, You give him an understanding of Your Word; that as long as he seeks You, You will prosper him. Lord, have pleasure in the prosperity of my husband for he is Your servant.

2 Chronicles 26:5; Psalm 35:27

*I*n my husband's time of financial need, I pray he will seek You and find that You have already given him the power to prosper, to receive wealth and riches. Thank You for sending his provision immediately.

Psalm 118:25; Deuteronomy 8:18

*F*ather, Proverbs 13:22 states that *"the wealth of the sinner is laid up for the just"* (KJV) and that, because of the blood of Jesus, my husband is a justified man who qualifies for the transfer of wealth. I declare he will enjoy and share his wealth with others.

Ecclesiastes 5:19

I pray my husband becomes acquainted with the grace of our Lord and Savior Jesus Christ, who was rich, yet for my husband's sake became poor. Through Your poverty, my husband has become rich. Thank You that Your blessings make him rich and add no sorrow with it.

2 Corinthians 8:9; Proverbs 10:22

ather, I declare my husband lives as a tree, planted by rivers of water, that brings forth fruit in its season and his leaf does not wither, but whatever he does prospers.

Psalm 1:3

declare my husband will keep Your statutes and commands so he may multiply greatly, prosper, and live long in the land You have given to us for all time. Teach him to instruct our children to follow Your ways and walk in obedience so they can prosper and live long lives in the land You have given us to possess.

Deuteronomy 4:40, 5:29, 6:3

Chapter 8

MY HUSBAND'S
DELIVERANCE

*There are scores of individuals within the body of Christ
who struggle with various forms of addictions and
habits. Notice I did not say individuals in the world,
but rather individuals within the body of Christ—the
church. Satan, through our ignorance of the Word of
God and our unwillingness to say no to our flesh, has
brought great trouble to many marriages. Nevertheless,
there is hope. Through prayer, we can break the powers
of darkness hovering over the lives of our husbands.
There is liberty and freedom from every form of bondage,
no matter what the problem is or how old it is. God has
the answer, and He is more than willing to release His
power so that our husbands can live their lives free from
the bondages inflicted by Satan.*

Father, Jesus declared, "The Spirit of the LORD is upon
Me, because He has anointed Me to preach the gos-
pel to the poor; He has sent Me to heal the brokenhearted, to
proclaim liberty to the captives and recovery of sight to the

blind, to set at liberty those who are oppressed." Thank You for delivering my husband over two thousand years ago from anything that would ever try to bind him.

Luke 4:18

Thank You for being a hiding place for my husband, may he always know You as his deliverer and pre- server. Encompass him with songs of deliverance so he can always trust in You when he is afraid. You have delivered him from the evil one and every evil spirit that comes to steal, kill, or destroy his life.

Psalm 32:7; John 10:10

Give my husband the wisdom to know that prayer and Your Word will continually deliver him out of every temptation as he walks in Your way. Thank You that he will call upon You—and not man—when he needs deliverance in his life.

Matthew 6:13; 2 Peter 2:9; Psalm 22:4–5

Father, when my husband sets his love upon You, deliver him and set him on high because he has become intimately acquainted with Your name.

Psalm 91:14–15

Deliver my husband from evil people, those who speak perverse things, and from the immoral woman. I pray against the words of the flattering seductress, those who would draw my husband away from the will and pur- pose You have for him.

Proverbs 2:12–16

My Husband's *Deliverance*

*L*ord, when my husband struggles with doing right or wrong, I declare he will overcome and win the war over his flesh, for this I thank You.

Romans 7:15–25

*T*hank You that my husband was once dead, but he trusted in You and You raised him from the dead. You delivered him from *"so great a death."* Currently You are delivering him from every circumstance and will continue to be his deliverer as long as he trusts in You.

2 Corinthians 1:7–10

*G*ive my husband the strength to refuse to submit to ungodly desires or passions, for Your Word says that every man is tempted when he is drawn away from You by his own desires and enticement. I pray he lives his life walking close to You. Draw my husband away from evil activities—pornography, adultery, homosexuality, or any other form of sexual immorality. I declare my husband will stay away from ungodly desires because his heart is committed to You.

James 1:14; 2 Timothy 4:18

Chapter 9

MY HUSBAND'S LIFE IN CHRIST

When my husband made a serious decision to dedicate his life to Christ, he had been in church all of his life. Unfortunately he lacked knowledge of who he was in Christ. Because of his prayer life and his dedication to the Word of God, his life began to change dramatically. God's desire is to have Christ formed in the lives of our husbands. When we pray for our husbands, God moves on our behalf and the desire increases for more of Him within their lives.

Father, give my husband the strength to do all that is written in Your Word. I pray he never turns aside from Your Word. Give him Your courage in all that he does, strengthen him and let him be bold in his walk with You.

Joshua 23:6; 1:8

Lord, perfect his life, not as I desire, but according to Your Word. You are the one who works in his life to do

Your good pleasure; complete the good work You have begun in his life until the day of Christ.

Psalm 138:8; Philippians 4:13, 1:6

*Y*ou, dear Father, are the potter, and my husband is the clay in your hands. He is your workmanship in Christ Jesus, created for good works. You have ordained his life. My husband was fashioned and formed to do Your works and those of Your kingdom.

Jeremiah 18:6; Ephesians 2:10

*M*ake my husband a vessel of honor, sanctified and useful for Your use. Thank You for making him a man of God, complete and equipped for every good work. As a servant of Christ, I labor fervently for my husband in prayer that he *"may stand perfect and complete in all the will of God."*

2 Timothy 2:21, 3:17; Colossians 4:12

*P*erfect my husband's heart in You, Lord, as he walks in Your statutes and keeps Your commandments. Give him the help he needs to behave himself wisely. I declare my husband will not look at the things that are behind him, but look ahead and press toward the mark for the prize of the high calling of God, which is in Christ Jesus, our Lord.

Ezekiel 20:19; Psalm 101:2; Philippians 3:12–14

I thank You that my husband was buried with Christ by baptism into His death and, like Christ, was raised from the dead by Your glory. I pray he walk in newness of life. As he walks after the Spirit and not his flesh, I pray he remembers

there is now no condemnation for those in Christ Jesus because You have made him free from the law of sin and death.

Romans 6:4, 8:1–2

*O*pen my husband's eyes so he can see and know that the Spirit who raised Jesus from the dead dwells in him. That same Spirit gives life to my husband by dwelling in him.

Romans 8:11

*L*ord, I pray my husband lives in such a way that his good will not be spoken of as evil. I pray he serves Christ with his life, that he is acceptable to You and approved of men. I declare my husband pursues the things that make for peace and that edify others.

Romans 14:16–19

*L*ord, I thank and praise You for the grace that You have given to my husband, by Jesus Christ. Through Your grace, You enrich my husband in everything, in all utterance and all knowledge. Just like the testimony of Christ was confirmed in him, he lacks in no gift waiting for the coming of our Lord Jesus Christ.

1 Corinthians 1:7

I pray my husband speaks the same things as those who have dedicated themselves to the Word of God and are known by the name of our Lord Jesus Christ. Let there be no division between my husband and his peers. He needs to be perfectly joined together in the same mind and in the same judgment.

1 Corinthians 1:10

ather, I thank You that Christ was made wisdom, righteousness, sanctification, and redemption in my husband's life. Thank You for establishing my husband and anointing him in Christ.

1 Corinthians 1:30; 2 Corinthians 1:21

ord, I thank You that You always cause my husband to triumph in Christ, and You make known the delight of Your knowledge by him everywhere he goes.

2 Corinthians 2:14

ord, open my husband's eyes so he can see that he is manifestly declared to be the epistle of Christ, written not with ink but by the Spirit of the living God; not in tablets of stone, but on tablets of flesh of the heart. I pray he remembers that one day he will appear before the judgment seat of Christ and he will receive the things done in his body according to what he has done, whether good or bad.

2 Corinthians 3:3, 5:10

pray my husband never holds on to his past because he is in Christ and is a new creation. Old things have passed away and all things are new. You have made him an ambassador for Christ, and his mission is to reconcile others to You.

2 Corinthians 5:17, 20

o not allow my husband to be deceived by the devil's subtlety, as Eve was, or his mind led astray from the simplicity that is in Christ. He is crucified with Christ; nevertheless, it is no longer he who lives, but Christ lives in him. The life he now lives in the flesh, he lives by faith in the Son of God who loved him and gave Himself for him.

2 Corinthians 11:3; Galatians 2:20

Father, I thank You that, in Christ, You have blessed my husband with all spiritual blessings in heavenly places. You made him the praise of Your glory because he trusted in You. Even when my husband was dead in sin, You made him alive together with Christ and saved him by grace. Thank You for showing the exceeding riches of Your grace in Your kindness toward my husband through Christ Jesus. My husband is Your workmanship, created in Christ Jesus for good works, which You prepared beforehand that he should walk in them. Thank You for drawing my husband near You by the blood of Christ.

Ephesians 1:3, 12; 2:5, 7, 10, 13

Chapter 10

MY HUSBAND'S HUNGER
FOR THE WORD

Psalm 119 is one of my many favorites because it reveals something that every believer should have— a heart that longs for the Word of God. I have used these Scriptures for years, praying them for my husband, and today I can see the fruit of my prayers.

I have divided selected verses into thirty-one prayers, one for each day of the month, using the New Living Translation. Read one each day and watch as God creates an insatiable hunger in your husband for His Word.

Day 1

Joyful are people of integrity, who follow the instructions of the LORD. Joyful are those who obey his laws and search for him with all their hearts. They do not compromise with evil, and they walk only in his paths. You have charged us to keep your commandments carefully. Oh, that my actions would consistently reflect your decrees! Then I will not be ashamed when I compare my life with your commands.

(Psalm 119:1–6 NLT)

Father, I declare that my husband is a man of integrity, a man who follows Your law. He obeys Your decrees and searches for You with all his heart. Thank You that he will not compromise with evil and walks only in Your paths. You have charged him to keep Your commandments carefully. Oh, that my husband's actions would consistently reflect Your principles. Then, he will not be disgraced when he compares his life with Your commands.

Day 2

As I learn your righteous regulations, I will thank you by living as I should! I will obey your decrees. Please don't give up on me! How can a young person stay pure? By obeying your word. I have tried hard to find you—don't let me wander from your commands. I have hidden your word in my heart, that I might not sin against you. I praise you, O Lord; teach me your decrees. I have recited aloud all the regulations you have given us. I have rejoiced in your laws as much as in riches. (Psalm 119:7–14 NLT)

I thank You that as my husband learns Your righteous laws, he will honor You by living his life as he should, obeying Your principles. I praise and thank You that You will not give up on my husband. Keep him pure as he obeys Your Word and follows its rules. I pray You do not allow him to wander from Your commands because he has found You. Hide Your Word in his heart that he might not sin against You. Teach him Your principles, open his mouth, and cause him to recite aloud all the laws You have given in Your Word. Let him rejoice in Your decrees as much as he would in riches.

Day 3

I will study your commandments and reflect on your ways. I will delight in your decrees and not forget your word. Be good to your servant, that I may live and obey your word. Open my eyes to see the wonderful truths in your instructions. I am only a foreigner in the land. Don't hide your commands from me!

(Psalm 119:15–19 NLT)

Lord, I believe and pray that my husband will study Your commandments and reflect on Your ways. He will delight in Your principles and not forget Your Word. Be good to my husband for he is Your servant, that he can live and obey Your commandments. Open his eyes to see the wonderful truths in Your law. I pray he understands he is just a foreigner here on earth and he needs the guidance of Your commands. Thank You that You will not hide them from him.

Day 4

I am always overwhelmed with a desire for your regulations. You rebuke the arrogant; those who wander from your commands are cursed. Don't let them scorn and insult me, for I have obeyed your laws. Even princes sit and speak against me, but I will meditate on your decrees. Your laws please me; they give me wise advice. I lie in the dust; revive me by your word. I told you my plans, and you answered. Now teach me your decrees. Help me understand the meaning of your commandments, and I will meditate on your wonderful deeds. I weep with sorrow; encourage me by your word. Keep me from lying to myself; give me the privilege of knowing your instructions.

(Psalm 119:20–29 NLT)

Father, overwhelm my husband continually with a desire for Your laws. I know You rebuke those who are too proud and wander away from Your commandments. Do not let this happen to my husband. Do not allow the proud to scorn and insult my husband, because he has obeyed Your decrees. Thank You that even when leaders sit and speak against him, he will meditate on Your principles. Let Your Word please my husband and give him wise advice. When he is overwhelmed and completely discouraged, revive him by Your Word. When he weeps with grief, encourage him by Your Word. Keep my husband from lying to himself; give him the privilege of knowing your law.

Day 5

I have chosen to be faithful; I have determined to live by your regulations. I cling to your laws. LORD, don't let me be put to shame! I will pursue your commands, for you expand my understanding. Teach me your decrees, O LORD; I will keep them to the end. Give me understanding and I will obey your instructions; I will put them into practice with all my heart.

(Psalm 119:30–34 NLT)

I pray my husband tells You of his plans, and I thank You for answering him. Teach him Your principles; I pray he understands the meaning of Your commandments and meditates on Your wonderful miracles. Give him a determination to live by Your law. Give him the strength to cling to Your decrees. Do not allow him to be put to shame. I pray he runs to follow Your commands. Teach him to follow every one of Your principles. Give him understanding and he will obey Your law; he will put it into practice with all his heart.

Day 6

Make me walk along the path of your commands, for that is where my happiness is found. Give me an eagerness for your laws rather than a love for money! Turn my eyes from worthless things, and give me life through your word. Reassure me of your promise, made to those who fear you. Help me abandon my shameful ways; for your regulations are good.

(Psalm 119:35–39 NLT)

*L*ord, I pray my husband walks along the path of Your commands, for this is where his happiness is found. Give him an eagerness for Your decrees. Do not allow him to become infatuated with the love for money; turn his eyes from worthless things and give him life through Your Word. Reassure him of Your promise, which is for those who honor You. I declare he will abandon his shameful, ungodly ways so that Your laws are all he wants in life.

Day 7

I long to obey your commandments! Renew my life with your goodness. LORD, give me your unfailing love, the salvation that you promised me. Then I can answer those who taunt me, for I trust in your word. Do not snatch your word of truth from me, for your regulations are my only hope. I will keep on obeying your instructions forever and ever.

(Psalm 119:40–44 NLT)

I pray for a hunger in my husband so he longs to obey Your commandment. Renew his life with Your goodness. Thank You for giving him Your unfailing love, which is manifested through the plan of salvation You promised and gave to him. Give my husband an answer for those who taunt him because he trusts in Your Word. Thank You that you will never snatch Your word of truth from my husband because his only hope is in Your law. I pray he will continue obeying Your law, forever.

Day 8

I will walk in freedom, for I have devoted myself to your commandments. I will speak to kings about your laws, and I will not be ashamed. How I delight in your commands! How I love them! I honor and love your commands. I meditate on your decrees.

(Psalm 119:45–48 NLT)

Heavenly Father, I thank You that my husband will walk in freedom because he has devoted himself to Your commandments. Open doors of opportunities and he will speak to kings about Your decrees; he will not be ashamed. I pray he delights in Your commands and falls in love them. I pray he honors and meditates on Your principles every single day.

Day 9

*Remember your promise to me; it is my only hope.
Your promise revives me; it comforts me in all my
troubles. The proud hold me in utter contempt, but
I do not turn away from your instructions. I meditate on your age-old regulations; O LORD, they comfort me.* (Psalm 119:49–52 NLT)

Lord, remember Your promise to my husband, for it is his only hope. Your promise revives him; it comforts him in his afflictions. The proud will try to hold him in utter contempt, but he will not turn away from Your law. Thank You that my husband meditates on Your age-old laws and they comfort him.

Day 10

*Your decrees have been the theme of my songs wher-
ever I have lived. I reflect at night on who you are, O
Lord; therefore, I obey your instructions. This is how
I spend my life: obeying your commandments. Lord,
you are mine! I promise to obey your words!*

(Psalm 119:54–57 NLT)

Make Your principles the music of my husband's life
throughout the years of his pilgrimage on this earth. I
pray he reflects at night on who You are, and obeys Your law
because of his reflections. Let this be my husband's happy
way of life: obeying Your commandments. You are his help
in keeping his promise to obey Your words.

Day 11

With all my heart I want your blessings. Be merciful as you promised. I pondered the direction of my life, and I turned to follow your laws. I will hurry, without delay, to obey your commands. Evil people try to drag me into sin, but I am firmly anchored to your instructions. I rise at midnight to thank you for your just regulations. I am a friend to anyone who fears you—anyone who obeys your commandments.

(Psalm 119:58–63 NLT)

Father, my husband's heart wants Your blessings. Be merciful just as You promised. I pray that my husband ponders the direction of his life and turns to follow Your statutes. I pray he hurries, without lingering, to obey Your commands. When evil people try to drag my husband into sin, make him firmly anchored to Your law. At midnight, let him rise to thank You for Your just laws. Let his friends be those who fear You, those who obey Your Word.

Day 12

O Lord, your unfailing love fills the earth; teach me your decrees. You have done many good things for me, Lord, just as you promised. I believe in your commands; now teach me good judgment and knowledge. I used to wander off until you disciplined me; but now I closely follow your word. You are good and do only good; teach me your decrees.

(Psalm 119:64–68 NLT)

*L*ord, the earth is full of Your unfailing love; teach my husband Your principles of love. You have done many good things for him, just as You promised. I believe in Your commands; now teach my husband good judgment and knowledge. I pray You will discipline my husband so that he will not wander off; instead, he will closely follow Your Word. You are good and do only good; teach him Your principles.

Day 13

Arrogant people smear me with lies, but in truth I obey your commandments with all my heart. Their hearts are dull and stupid, but I delight in your instructions. My suffering was good for me, for it taught me to pay attention to your decrees. Your instructions are more valuable to me than millions in gold and silver.

(Psalm 119:69–72 NLT)

Father, when arrogant people have made up lies about my husband, I pray he remains in truth and obeys Your commandments with all his heart. Their hearts may be dull of understanding, but he delights in Your law. Thank You that any suffering my husband endures teaches him to pay attention to Your principles. Make Your law more valuable to my husband than millions in gold and silver.

Day 14

*You made me; you created me. Now give me the sense
to follow your commands. May all who fear you find
in me a cause for joy, for I have put my hope in your
word. I know, O LORD, that your regulations are fair;
you disciplined me because I needed it. Now let your
unfailing love comfort me, just as you promised me,
your servant. Surround me with your tender mercies
so I may live, for your instructions are my delight.*

(Psalm 119:73–77 NLT)

ord, You made my husband; You created him. Give him
the sense to follow Your commands. I know Your decisions are fair; You discipline my husband because he needs
it. Let Your unfailing love comfort him, just as You promised
in Your Word. He is Your servant. Surround him with Your
tender mercies so he may live. Make Your law his delight.

Day 15

Let me be united with all who fear you, with those who know your laws. May I be blameless in keeping your decrees; then I will never be ashamed. I am worn out waiting for your rescue, but I have put my hope in your word. My eyes are straining to see your promises come true. When will you comfort me?

(Psalm 119:79–82 NLT)

Let my husband be reconciled with all who fear You and know Your decrees. May he be blameless in keeping Your principles, then he will never have to be ashamed. I pray my husband will faint with longing for Your salvation; when he puts hope in Your Word, You satisfy him. Allow him to strain his eyes because he is engulfed in viewing Your promises and seeing them come true. Thank You for answering him.

Day 16

I am shriveled like a wineskin in the smoke, but I have not forgotten to obey your decrees. How long must I wait? When will you punish those who persecute me? These arrogant people who hate your instructions have dug deep pits to trap me. All your commands are trustworthy. Protect me from those who hunt me down without cause. They almost finished me off, but I refused to abandon your commandments.

(Psalm 119:83–87 NLT)

Father, thank You for the days my husband is exhausted, waiting as he clings to Your principles and obeys them. If there is any arrogant person who hates Your law and has dug deep pits for my husband to fall into, I ask You to send a laborer across the path of that individual so they may come to know You, intimately and personally. May they come to know that all Your commands are worthy of trust. Protect him from those who hunt him down without cause. They desire to harm him; I pray he refuses to abandon Your commandments.

Day 17

In your unfailing love, spare my life; then I can continue to obey your laws. Your eternal word, O LORD, stands firm in heaven. Your faithfulness extends to every generation, as enduring as the earth you created. Your regulations remain true to this day, for everything serves your plans. (Psalm 119:88–91 NLT)

In Your unfailing love, You have spared my husband's life; may he continue to obey Your decrees. I pray he never forgets that Your Word stands firm in heaven forever. Your faithfulness extends to every generation, as enduring as the earth You created. Your laws remain true today, for everything serves Your plans.

Day 18

If your instructions hadn't sustained me with joy, I would have died in my misery. I will never forget your commandments, for by them you give me life. I am yours; rescue me! For I have worked hard at obeying your commandments. Though the wicked hide along the way to kill me, I will quietly keep my mind on your laws. (Psalm 119:92–95 NLT)

Thank You, Lord, that Your law sustains my husband with joy so he will not die in his misery. Do not let him ever forget Your commandments, for You have used them to restore his joy and health. My husband is Yours; You saved him. I declare he will apply himself to obey Your commandments. Even if the wicked hide along the way to destroy him, I pray he will quietly keep his mind on Your decrees.

Day 19

Even perfection has its limits, but your commands have no limit. Oh, how I love your instructions! I think about them all day long. Your commands make me wiser than my enemies, for they are my constant guide. Yes, I have more insight than my teachers, for I am always thinking of your laws. I am even wiser than my elders, for I have kept your commandments.
(Psalm 119:96–100 NLT)

I pray my husband will see that even perfection has its limits, but Your commands have no limit. Give him a love for Your law and help him think about it all day long. Your commands make him wiser than his enemies, and they are his constant guide. Give him more insight than his teachers when he is always thinking of Your decrees. Make him even wiser than his elders, when he has kept Your commandments.

Day 20

I have refused to walk on any evil path, so that I may remain obedient to your word. I haven't turned away from your regulations, for you have taught me well. How sweet your words taste to me; they are sweeter than honey. Your commandments give me understanding; no wonder I hate every false way of life. Your word is a lamp to guide my feet and a light for my path. (Psalm 119:101–105 NLT)

Father, I pray my husband refuses to walk on any path of evil, that he remain obedient to Your Word. Teach him well so he does not turn away from Your laws. Make Your Word sweet to his taste, sweeter than honey. I pray he hates every false way of life; give him understanding when he feeds on Your Word, because Your Word is a lamp for his feet and a light for his path.

Day 21

I've promised it once, and I'll promise it again: I will obey your righteous regulations. I have suffered much, O LORD; restore my life again as you promised. LORD, accept my offering of praise, and teach me your regulations. My life constantly hangs in the balance, but I will not stop obeying your instructions. The wicked have set their traps for me, but I will not turn from your commandments. Your laws are my treasure; they are my heart's delight. I am determined to keep your decrees to the very end.

(Psalm 119:106–112 NLT)

Father, I declare my husband will make a covenant with You concerning Your Word and he will know Your wonderful law. In the times of my husband's suffering, restore his life and health again as You promised in Your Word. Accept his grateful thanks and teach him Your law. When his life is uncertain, help him focus and never stop obeying Your law. I pray against the traps of the wicked that are set along his path; may he never turn from Your Word. Let Your decrees be my husband's treasure and his heart's delight. I declare he will determine to keep Your principles, forever.

Day 22

I hate those with divided loyalties, but I love your instructions. You are my refuge and my shield; your word is my source of hope. Get out of my life, you evil-minded people, for I intend to obey the commands of my God. LORD, sustain me as you promised, that I may live! Do not let my hope be crushed. Sustain me, and I will be rescued; then I will meditate continually on your decrees. (Psalm 119:113–117 NLT)

Keep my husband away from those who are undecided about You, and should he spend time with them, may he be the one to influence them. I declare his choice will always be clear because my husband's love is Your law. Father, You are my husband's refuge and his shield; Your Word is his only source of hope. Remove evil-minded people from his life, for he intends to obey the commands of his God. Lord, sustain my husband as You promised, so he can live. Do not let his hope be crushed for he will be saved. He will meditate on Your principles continually.

Day 23

But you have rejected all who stray from your decrees. They are only fooling themselves. You skim off the wicked of the earth like scum; no wonder I love to obey your laws! I tremble in fear of you; I stand in awe of your regulations. Don't leave me to the mercy of my enemies, for I have done what is just and right. Please guarantee a blessing for me. Don't let the arrogant oppress me! (Psalm 119:118–122 NLT)

Lord, You reject all who stray from your principles for they are only fooling themselves. Do not allow my husband to reject Your law and become self-deceived. All the wicked of the earth are the hopeless; I pray my husband loves obeying Your decrees. I pray my husband trembles in fear of You and that he fears Your judgment. I declare my husband reverences and respects Your Word. Thank You that when he has done what is right; You will not leave him to the mercy of his enemies. Guarantee a blessing for my husband and do not let those who are arrogant oppress him.

Day 24

My eyes strain to see your rescue, to see the truth of your promise fulfilled. I am your servant; deal with me in unfailing love, and teach me your decrees. Give discernment to me, your servant; then I will understand your laws. LORD, it is time for you to act, for these evil people have violated your instructions. Truly, I love your commands more than gold, even the finest gold. Each of your commandments is right. That is why I hate every false way.

(Psalm 119:123–128 NLT)

Lord, my eyes strain to see Your deliverance in my husband's life and the truth of Your promise fulfilled in him. He is Your servant; deal with him in unfailing love and teach him Your principles. Give him discernment so he will understand Your decrees. When it is time for judgment to come in the lives of those around my husband who have broken Your law, help him pray for mercy on their behalf. I pray my husband will hate every false way and truly love Your commands more than gold, even the finest gold. For each of Your commandments is right.

Day 25

Your laws are wonderful. No wonder I obey them! The teaching of your word gives light, so even the simple can understand. I pant with expectation, longing for your commands. Come and show me your mercy, as you do for all who love your name. Guide my steps by your word, so I will not be overcome by evil. Ransom me from the oppression of evil people; then I can obey your commandments. Look upon me with love; teach me your decrees. (Psalm 119:129–135 NLT)

Lord, Your decrees are wonderful and my husband obeys them. Thank You that as Your words are taught, they give light and are simple enough that my husband can understand them. Open his mouth, help him pant in expectancy, longing for Your commands. Thank You that Your mercy is shown in my husband's life because he loves Your name. Guide his steps by Your Word, and he will not be overcome by evil. Rescue him from the oppression of evil people because he obeys Your commandments. Thank You for looking down on my husband with love; teach him all Your principles.

Day 26

Rivers of tears gush from my eyes because people disobey your instructions. O LORD, you are righteous, and your regulations are fair. Your laws are perfect and completely trustworthy. I am overwhelmed with indignation, for my enemies have disregarded your words. Your promises have been thoroughly tested; that is why I love them so much. I am insignificant and despised, but I don't forget your commandments. Your justice is eternal, and your instructions are perfectly true. (Psalm 119:136–142 NLT)

Give my husband a heart of sensitivity toward You so rivers of tears flow from his eyes when he observes people disobeying Your law. When Your Word is disregarded, I pray he is overwhelmed with rage. O Lord, You are righteous and Your decisions are fair. Your decrees are perfect; they are entirely worthy of our trust. Your promises have been thoroughly tested; that is why I love them so much. When my husband feels insignificant and despised, do not allow him to forget Your commandments. May he remember that Your justice is eternal and Your law is perfectly true.

Day 27

As pressure and stress bear down on me, I find joy
in your commands. Your laws are always right; help
me to understand them so I may live. I pray with all
my heart; answer me, LORD! I will obey your decrees.
I cry out to you; rescue me, that I may obey your laws.
I rise early, before the sun is up; I cry out for help and
put my hope in your words. I stay awake through the
night, thinking about your promise. In your faithful
love, O LORD, hear my cry; let me be revived by follow-
ing your regulations. (Psalm 119:143–149 NLT)

ather, when pressure and stress bear down on my
husband, I pray he finds joy in Your commands.
Your decrees are always fair; I pray he understands them
so he may live. When my husband prays with all his heart,
thank You for answering him. He will obey Your principles.
When he cries out to You, save him so that he may obey Your
decrees. Place it in my husband's heart to rise early, before
the sun is up, and cry out to You for help; may he put his
hope in Your words. I ask that when he stays awake through
the night, cause him to think about Your promise. In Your
faithful love, O Lord, hear my husband's cry; in Your justice,
save his life.

Day 28

Lawless people are coming to attack me; they live far from your instructions. But you are near, O LORD, and all your commands are true. I have known from my earliest days that your laws will last forever. Look upon my suffering and rescue me, for I have not forgotten your instructions. Argue my case; take my side! Protect my life as you promised. The wicked are far from rescue, for they do not bother with your decrees. LORD, how great is your mercy; let me be revived by following your regulations. Many persecute and trouble me, yet I have not swerved from your laws. Seeing these traitors makes me sick at heart, because they care nothing for your word. (Psalm 119:150–158 NLT)

Lord, do not allow my husband to fear lawless people who may attack him, those who live far from Your law. I pray he always remembers You are near and Your commandments to protect him are true. I have known from my earliest days that Your decrees never change. So, look down upon my husband's sorrows and rescue him, for I have not forgotten Your law. Thank You for allowing me to argue his case and for taking my side. Thank You for protecting my husband's life as You promised. My husband prays for those who care nothing for Your Word, who are far from salvation, and those who do not bother with Your principles.

Day 29

See how I love your commandments, Lord. Give back my life because of your unfailing love. The very essence of your words is truth; all your just regulations will stand forever. Powerful people harass me without cause, but my heart trembles only at your word. I rejoice in your word like one who discovers a great treasure. (Psalm 119:159–162 NLT)

Lord, how great is Your mercy. In Your justice, give my husband back his life. Many have persecuted and troubled my husband, but give him grace so he will not swerve from Your decrees. All Your words are true; all Your just laws will stand forever. When powerful people harass my husband without cause, help his heart to only tremble at Your Word. I declare he rejoices in Your Word like one who finds a great treasure.

Day 30

I hate and abhor all falsehood, but I love your instructions. I will praise you seven times a day because all your regulations are just. Those who love your instructions have great peace and do not stumble. I long for your rescue, LORD, so I have obeyed your commands. I have obeyed your laws, for I love them very much. Yes, I obey your commandments and laws because you know everything I do. O LORD, listen to my cry; give me the discerning mind you promised.

(Psalm 119:163–169 NLT)

Father, I pray that my husband hates and abhors all falsehood, but loves Your law. May my husband praise You seven times a day because all Your laws are just. Thank You, because he loves Your law; he has great peace and does not stumble. May he long for Your salvation, Lord, and obey Your commands. I pray he obeys Your decrees, and loves them very much. Yes, I pray he obeys Your commandments and decrees because You know everything that he does. Oh Lord, listen to my husband's cry; give him the discerning mind You promised.

Day 31

Listen to my prayer; rescue me as you promised. Let praise flow from my lips, for you have taught me your decrees. Let my tongue sing about your word, for all your commands are right. Give me a helping hand, for I have chosen to follow your commandments. O LORD, I have longed for your rescue, and your instructions are my delight. Let me live so I can praise you, and may your regulations help me. I have wandered away like a lost sheep; come and find me, for I have not forgotten your commands.

(Psalm 119:170–176 NLT)

Lord, listen to my husband's prayer; rescue him as You promised. Let his lips burst forth with praise because You have taught him Your principles. Let his tongue sing about Your Word, for all Your commands are right. Thank You, because You stand ready to help my husband, for he has chosen to follow Your commandments. I pray he longs for Your salvation; may Your law be his delight. Give him a long life so he can praise You; let Your law sustain him. Should my husband wander away like a lost sheep, find him, for he has not forgotten Your commands.

Chapter 11

MY HUSBAND'S PROTECTION

*Because my husband travels constantly, I am always
prayingfor his safety and protection. Threats of
terrorism and various weather conditions will try
to instill fear and dread. But I am confident in the
blood of Jesus, which hovers over my husband,
and I can pray from a place of rest knowing
God watches over him for me.*

Father, You are my husband's protection; the blood
of Jesus covers his life just as it did the people
of Israel under the old covenant. Psalm 91 is a very real
promise from You to my husband. Thank You that he will
always dwell in Your secret place. Because he does, he
abides under Your shadow for You are the almighty One.
Let him say You are his refuge and his fortress; he trust
in You.

Thank You for delivering him from the pestilence, for
covering him with Your wings and truth for You are his
shield and buckler. He will not be afraid of the terror by

night or the arrow that flies by day, for You are his refuge. A thousand may fall at his side and ten thousand at his right hand, but it shall not come near him.

Because my husband has made You his refuge, even You, the most High God, his dwelling place, no evil shall befall him and no plagues shall come near him. Thank You for giving Your angels charge over him, to keep him in all Your ways. The angels shall bear my husband up in their hands. Thank You for protecting his life under Your divine covering.

Psalm 91:1–12

*L*ord, I agree that no weapon formed against my husband will prosper and that You will condemn every tongue that raises against him. Thank You that he does not have to fight his own battles, but You will fight them for him.

Isaiah 54:17

*Y*ou created my husband, You formed him, You redeemed him, and he is Yours—he belongs to You. He does not have to fear because when he passes through the rivers they shall not overflow him. When he passes through the fire, he shall not be burned. For You are the Lord his God.

Isaiah 43:1

*S*atan may desire to sift my husband as he did the apostle Peter, but I pray for him just as Jesus prayed for Peter, that my husband's faith will not fail him.

Luke 22:31–32

$\mathcal{A}$s my husband keeps the Word of God before his eyes and within his mouth, wisdom and discretion shall rest upon him; his foot shall not stumble, he will not be afraid. He shall be restful; he will not be fearful. You will keep his foot from being taken.

Proverbs 4:20–21; 3:23

$\mathcal{F}$ather, my husband needs wisdom for his life. Thank You that he does not lack wisdom because You liberally give it to him. Preserve my husband from violent men, those whose purpose is to overthrow his efforts. Keep him in perfect peace as he keeps his mind on You.

James 1:5; Isaiah 26:3

Chapter 12

MY HUSBAND'S LOVING NATURE

It is through love and kindness that Jesus draws us to Himself. With this same spirit of love, we are to draw others to Christ. After submitting himself to the Word of God, and through many seasons of prayer, I can truly say that my husband is committed to living his life in the love of God.

ather, I pray my husband loves You with all his heart, with all his soul, and with all his mind. Let him show his love toward You by keeping Your commandments. I pray he honors his father and mother; help him love his neighbor as he does himself. Give him the grace to love his enemies, to bless those who curse him, to do good to those who hate him, and to pray for those who spitefully use and persecute him.

Matthew 19:19, 22:37, 5:44; John 14:14

pray iniquity does not abound in my husband's life so the love in him never grows cold. Let the love in him manifest to others so the world can see and know that he is one of Your disciples. Let his love be proven to You, give him

a heart to lay his life down for his friends. Let him be kindly affectionate to another with brotherly love—honoring, serving, and preferring others.

I pray my husband owes no man, except to love them. Never allow him to work ill toward his neighbor so he can walk in the fulfillment of the law You have given to him

Matthew 24:12; John 13:35, 15:13;
Galatians 5:13; Romans 13:8, 10

Thank You that my husband is a man who has Your commandments, and keeps them. He loves You and You love him; manifest Yourself to him. Reveal Yourself to my husband so that he can know You on a more intimate level. I pray he continues in Your love and allows that love to be without hiding; I pray he abhors evil and clings to what is good. Thank You that Your love in him constrains him and he speaks the truth in love no matter what the circumstance.

John 14:21, 15:9; Romans 12:9; 2 Corinthians 5:14;
Ephesians 4:15

1 Corinthians 13 (Amplified Bible)

There are many translations, but none gets to the heart of the thirteenth chapter of 1 Corinthians like the *Amplified Bible*. It reveals the true heart of God for the believer.

If I [can] speak in the tongues of men and [even] of angels, but have not love (that reasoning, intentional, spiritual devotion such as is inspired by God's love for and in us), I am only a noisy gong or a clanging

cymbal. And if I have prophetic powers (the gift of interpreting the divine will and purpose), and understand all the secret truths and mysteries and possess all knowledge, and if I have [sufficient] faith so that I can remove mountains, but have not love (God's love in me) I am nothing (a useless nobody). Even if I dole out all that I have [to the poor in providing] food, and if I surrender my body to be burned or in order that I may glory, but have not love (God's love in me), I gain nothing. Love endures long and is patient and kind; love never is envious nor boils over with jealousy, is not boastful or vainglorious, does not display itself haughtily. It is not conceited (arrogant and inflated with pride); it is not rude (unmannerly) and does not act unbecomingly. Love (God's love in us) does not insist on its own rights or its own way, for it is not self-seeking; it is not touchy or fretful or resentful; it takes no account of the evil done to it [it pays no attention to a suffered wrong]. It does not rejoice at injustice and unrighteousness, but rejoices when right and truth prevail. Love bears up under anything and everything that comes, is ever ready to believe the best of every person, its hopes are fadeless under all circumstances, and it endures everything [without weakening]. Love never fails [never fades out or becomes obsolete or comes to an end]. As for prophecy (the gift of interpreting the divine will and purpose), it will be fulfilled and pass away; as for tongues, they will be destroyed and cease; as for knowledge, it will pass away [it will lose its value and be superseded

by truth]. For our knowledge is fragmentary (incomplete and imperfect), and our prophecy (our teaching) is fragmentary (incomplete and imperfect). But when the complete and perfect (total) comes, the incomplete and imperfect will vanish away (become antiquated, void, and superseded). When I was a child, I talked like a child, I thought like a child, I reasoned like a child; now that I have become a man, I am done with childish ways and have put them aside. For now we are looking in a mirror that gives only a dim (blurred) reflection [of reality as in a riddle or enigma], but then [when perfection comes] we shall see in reality and face to face! Now I know in part (imperfectly), but then I shall know and understand fully and clearly, even in the same manner as I have been fully and clearly known and understood [by God]. And so faith, hope, love abide [faith—conviction and belief respecting man's relation to God and divine things; hope—joyful and confident expectation of eternal salvation; love—true affection for God and man, growing out of God's love for and in us], these three; but the greatest of these is love. (1 Corinthians 13 AMP)

Father, I thank You that Romans 5:5 states Your love *"has been poured out in our hearts by the Holy Spirit,"* so the love in my husband is active, real, and strong.

Thank You that the love in my husband endures and is patient and kind; it is never envious nor boils over with jealousy. The love in my husband will not allow him to be boastful or vainglorious, and it does not display itself arrogantly.

The love You have placed in my husband is not conceited (arrogant and inflated with pride); so my husband is not conceited, arrogant, or inflated with pride. My husband does not act in an unbecoming way, because Your love in him does not insist on its own rights or its own way; it is not self-seeking.

I pray my husband is not touchy, fretful, or resentful, and that he takes no account of an evil done to him; he pays no attention to a suffered wrong. My husband is quick to forgive. Your love in my husband does not rejoice at injustice and unrighteousness, but it rejoices when right and truth prevail.

Because of the love of God in him, my husband bears up under anything and everything that comes; he is ever ready to believe the best of every person.

I pray he is slow to speak concerning a brother or sister and swift to hear what You have to say about them.

Father, the love You have given him is fadeless and it hopes under all circumstances; it endures everything without weakening. Therefore, my husband can endure everything without weakening. Thank You for Your love in my husband's life.

Chapter 13

My Husband's Prayer Life

*In the early days of our marriage, my husband became
frustrated with his prayer life. He felt as though
his praying was ineffective. He always had a heart
toward God, but inevitably, prayer became a chore.
After praying with him, God began to teach my
husband the art of effective praying, and his life was
changed forever.*

*F*ather, thank You that You listen and respond to the
prayers of my husband, because it is to You that he
prays. Evening, morning, and at noon, give my husband a
heart to pray and cry aloud to You—and You will hear his
voice. Oh Lord, in the morning may he look up and direct his
prayer unto You.

Psalm 5:2–3, 55:17

*A*s Your servant David said, command Your loving-
kindness in the daytime, and in the night let Your
song be with my husband. Let his prayer be unto You, the
God of his life.

Psalm 42:8

*F*ather, I thank You my husband has a heart to draw near to You, and as he does, You draw near to him. Give him the things that are necessary for his life when he submits himself in prayer to You.

Hebrews 10:22

*T*hank You for hearing my husband's prayers and giving Your ear to the words of his mouth as he gives himself to prayer. Thank You for allowing him to come close to You. Let him lay aside the sin and weights of this world and seek Your face in prayer daily. You said You would forgive his sin and heal the land if he humbles himself and prays. Heal the land of my husband's life.

Psalm 109:4; Hebrews 12:1; 2 Chronicles 7:14

*F*ather, as Jesus understood the need to daily commune with You, I pray my husband keeps the same mind, for he needs You in his life. Thank You for placing a desire in his heart, a strong desire, to seek You in prayer. Teach my husband so that he will pray to You constantly. Do not allow him to faint or stop praying. When he calls, You always hear, and before he calls, You have already answered him. Keep this knowledge before him.

Mark 6:46; Isaiah 65:24; Luke 18:1

I pray my husband will not worry about anything, but in everything, through prayer and petition, with thanksgiving, he will make his request known to You. And Your peace, which surpasses every thought, will guard his heart and mind in Christ Jesus.

Philippians 4:6–7

My Husband's *Prayer Life*

*K*eep pride and vain repetitions out of my husband's prayer life. May he always pray in secret and allow You to reward him openly. Give him the heart to pray for his enemies and never seek revenge or justice, for You are his refuge. Open his eyes so he will see the nations and those within them just as You see them. When he sees the multitude, I pray he is moved with compassion as Jesus was. Increase his desire to pray that You send laborers into the harvest, while keeping Jerusalem in his prayers, thereby having great prosperity.

Matthew 5:44, 6:7, 9:38; Psalm 122:6

*W*hen my husband has a need, I pray he remembers the power in the Prayer of Agreement: *"that if two of you agree on earth concerning anything that they ask, it will be done for them by My Father in heaven"* (Matthew 18:19). I stand in agreement with my husband, and together, we expect Your answer. Open his eyes so he can see the power You have given him to call those things that be not as though they were, just as You do.

Romans 4:17

I pray my husband will speak the authoritative Word of God to mountains that may rise in our lives, business, or ministry, and see change for us as well as those around us. When his heart is overwhelmed, lead him to the rock that is higher than he is; that rock is You, Lord.

Mark 11:23–25; Psalm 61:2

*F*ather, when children came to Jesus, He laid His hands on them and blessed them. I pray my husband will invoke blessings upon our children and teach them to love You and our neighbors.

Matthew 19:13

103

ather, give my husband a mind to watch and pray because the days are evil. I pray he lives a life of prayer so when temptation comes, he will not enter into it. Thank You that the Spirit Himself helps my husband's weaknesses, for when he does not know what he should pray for, or the way he should pray, Your Spirit makes intercession for him with groanings that cannot be uttered in articulate speech.

Matthew 26:41; Romans 8:26

pray my husband sincerely desires spiritual gifts, so he can be a blessing to the body of Christ. Lord, I declare my husband prays and sings in the spirit and with his understanding. Give him the ability to interpret his prayer in tongues. I ask that the gifts of the Spirit manifest in my husband's life.

1 Corinthians 14:13–15

et him pray wherever he goes, lifting up holy hands without anger or without doubt, but fully trusting You. When my husband is afflicted, give him the strength to do his own praying. When he is happy, I pray he will sing unto You. When he is sick, let him call for the elders of the church and allow them to anoint him with oil in Your name. I thank You that he will be raised in health.

1 Timothy 2:8; James 5:14

ord, I pray when my husband makes a mistake he will confess his faults to the other person. I declare that the effectual fervent prayer of a righteous man makes tremendous power available to him.

James 5:16

Chapter 14

THE PRAYERS OF PAUL

*The prayers of Paul are some of the most profound
prayers found in the Word of God. These prayers are
good for every believer desiring to strengthen their
understanding of the Word of God, as well as His
plans and purposes. As you read them for your husband,
expect revelation knowledge to flow freely in his life,
and for him to grow in his spiritual walk with Christ.*

Father, I bow my knees unto You, the Father of Glory, that You would grant my husband the spirit of wisdom and revelation in the knowledge of You. Have the eyes of his understanding opened so he will know the hope of Your calling and the riches of the glory of Your inheritance in his life.

Ephesians 1:15–23

I pray my husband will know what the exceeding greatness of Your power is to him as a believer, according to the working of Your mighty power that You worked out in Your Son, Jesus Christ, when You raised Him from the dead and seated Him at Your own right hand.

You gave Your Son, Jesus, to be the head over all things to the church, and I honor Him as the head of my husband's life.

Ephesians 1:19–22

For this reason I bow my knees to the Father of our Lord Jesus Christ, from whom the whole family in heaven and earth is named, that He would grant you, according to the riches of His glory, to be strengthened with might through His Spirit in the inner man, that Christ may dwell in your hearts through faith; that you, being rooted and grounded in love, may be able to comprehend with all the saints what is the width and length and depth and height; to know the love of Christ which passes knowledge; that you may be filled with all the fullness of God.

(Ephesians 3:14–19)

Father, like Paul, I bow my knees unto You, the Father of my Lord, Jesus Christ, from whom the whole family in heaven and in earth is named.

Grant my husband, according to the riches of Your glory, to be strengthened with might by Your Spirit in his inner man. Let Christ dwell in my husband's heart by faith; that being rooted and grounded in love, he may be able to comprehend with all saints what is the width, length, depth, and height; and to know the love of Christ, which surpasses human knowledge. Fill my husband with Your fullness Father.

Father, I pray my husband's love, the love that was poured into his heart, *"may abound still more and more in knowledge and all discernment."* Let him approve the things that are excellent so he will be sincere and without offense until the day of Christ, *"being filled with the fruits of righteousness which are by Jesus Christ, to the glory and praise of God."*

Romans 5:5; Philippians 1:9–12

ather, I pray that my husband may be filled with the knowledge of Your will in all wisdom and spiritual understanding. That he walks worthy of You, fully pleasing You, and is fruitful in every good work and increasing in the knowledge of You.

I pray he is strengthened with all might, according to Your glorious power, for all patience and longsuffering with joy; giving thanks to You, who have qualified him to be a partaker of the inheritance of the saints in the light.

Colossians 1:9–12

Chapter 15

MY HUSBAND'S WALK

Many women find themselves consumed with the spiritual condition of their husbands. Early in our marriage, God taught me that He was the Lord over my husband's life, a job I would never hold. God showed me that He wanted to direct my husband's steps and that I needed to allow Him to do His job. Remember, God wants our husbands to walk with Him, and He also knows how to get them down the path of righteousness that He has mapped out.

Father, I thank You that my husband walks in the Spirit and does not fulfill the lust of his flesh. I pray he walks circumspectly, redeeming the time because the days are evil. Keep him from falling and present him faultless before the presence of Your glory with exceeding joy.

Galatians 5:16; Ephesians 5:15–16; Jude 24

Thank You that my husband trusts in You and that his life brings forth fruit that is fat and flourishing, even in his old age. I pray he walks worthy of You and is fully pleasing to You. Let him increase in the knowledge of You.

Thank You, for Your continual grace and favor is abounding toward my husband and he has sufficiency in all things. Do not allow him to get weary in doing good because You promised he would reap in due season if he does not lose heart.

Psalm 92:12–14; Colossians 1:10;
2 Corinthians 9:8; Galatians 6:9

Thank You for leading and guiding my husband into the truth of Your Word. Make Your voice clear so he will always know Your voice; You are his shepherd.

John 16:13, 10:14–16

Chapter 16

GUIDANCE FOR MY HUSBAND

As a young wife, I was trained to allow my husband to lead our family and make decisions. Often I became frustrated because I did not agree with all of his decisions, but I trusted God. Many times he made decisions that did not benefit us. But, I did not "ride" or ridicule him, I continued to pray and eventually he grew more and more sensitive to the leading of the Holy Spirit. As he did, his decision-making improved. Trust the Holy Spirit to lead and guide your husband. After all, Jesus said the Holy Spirit will lead you and "guide you into all truth" (John 16:13).

Father, I pray my husband trusts You with his whole heart and leans not on his own understanding. In all of his ways and decision-making he acknowledges You so that You can direct his path. Thank You for ordering his steps. May he not insist on planning his own way. Give him ears to hear Your voice. Do not allow him turn to the left or the right, but to look straight to Your Word. Show my husband great and mighty things that he does not know.

Proverbs 3:5–6; Psalm 37:23; Proverbs 16:9;
Deuteronomy 5:32; Jeremiah 33:3

Chapter 17

MY HUSBAND'S VICTORY

There is an age-old saying: "Behind every great man, there is a great woman." Ultimately, victory comes from living a righteous life and walking in obedience to the Word of God. But as wives, we play a major role in ensuring that our husbands walk in the victory Jesus has given them. Through praying the Word of God, we surround our husbands in an atmosphere of victory. The Word never fails, and when our husbands walk according to the Word of God, victory is inevitable.

$\mathcal{F}$ather, my husband walks in victory because You have called him to victory. Your Word declares he is steadfast, immovable, and always abounding in the work of the Lord.

1 Corinthians 15:57–58

$\mathcal{T}$hank You that my husband is born of You and, therefore, has the victory that overcomes the world. I pray he knows his work is not in vain as long as he is fulfilling Your will for his life.

1 John 5:4; 1 Corinthians 15:58

$\mathcal{F}$ ather, You are the greater One who indwells my husband. You are greater than the one who is in the world. Thank You that victory will manifest in his life and my husband has victory over the lust of flesh, the lust of eyes, the pride of life, and the works of the devil. I thank You my husband will not present himself as an instrument of unrighteousness. Thank You, Father, for my husband is more than a conqueror because You love him. My husband has victory over sin, it will not have dominion over his mortal body.

1 John 2:16, 4:4; Romans 6:13–14, 8:37

$\mathcal{T}$ hank You that my husband has received an abundance of grace and has been redeemed from the curse of the law. My husband has overcome by the blood of the Lamb and by the word of His testimony. May my husband's words always be words of faith and power.

Romans 5:17; Galatians 3:13; Revelation 12:11

Chapter 18

MY HUSBAND AND OUR HOME

For years, I worked diligently to make our home a place of rest and peace for my husband. While my husband is away, I spend time praying for him and our home; when he returns from his travels, I make certain that everything is clean and in order. I try to sweetly welcome him home, keeping away anything that saps his strength until he has rested. When he comes home, my husband knows that he will receive love, acceptance, and the appreciation he deserves as our family's provider. This attitude has aided in helping my husband keep our family as a priority in his life.

Father, give my husband the grace to rule our house well, and to teach our children submission with all dignity. I pray he submits himself to You and loves me as Christ loved the church. I thank You my husband rejoices in the wife of his youth and is still pleased to dwell with me and me alone.

1 Timothy 3:4; Ephesians 5:25; Proverbs 5:18

*T*hank You for Your favor on my husband's life because we are joined together. Give him the wisdom to prioritize our lives and position him to be a wonderful provider.

Proverbs 18:22; 1 Timothy 5:8

*T*hank You that my husband is slow to speak and swift to hear what You are saying to him concerning our marriage, our children, and our ministry. Give his heart the desire to teach our children to love You and Your Word. I pray he creates a desire in the heart of our children to walk in Your ways. Keep him from those things that draw him away from You, things that produce death in families.

James 1:19; Genesis 18:19; James 1:14

*T*hank You that my husband will not provoke our children to anger, but he tutors and trains them in the way they should go. I thank You my children will honor and respect him because he is a man of God.   *Ephesians 6:2, 4*

*T*hank You that my husband keeps his life submitted to the Word of God and to prayer so he always has wisdom to lead our family. I pray he honors You for the hedge of protection You have placed around our lives.

James 4:7; Job 1:10

I pray my children will see their father is a man of integrity who walks in righteousness in all that he does. Thank You that he is a strong example before our children, and for the sweet presence of Your Spirit who dwells in our home because of my husband's life. Thank You that my husband has taken his place as the priest of our home.

1 Kings 9:4; 1 Timothy 4:12; Acts 2:2

Chapter 19

MY HUSBAND'S CAREER

*It is essential that we hold to the practice of praying
for the success of our husbands' careers. No matter how
unimportant it may be to you, his achievement is very
important to him. Commit to praying for whatever
your husband sets his hand and heart to do.*

Father, thank You that wisdom and prudence rest deep in the heart of my husband. Just as King Solomon prayed for wisdom and knowledge so he could make godly judgments to lead Your people, grant my husband the wisdom and knowledge needed for success in his life of leadership. Fill his lips with knowledge as he regards discretion in his career and ministry. Give him wisdom and understanding far beyond his peers as he draws it daily from Your Word.

2 Chronicles 1:10; Proverbs 8:12, 5:2, 2:6

Thank You that my husband is a prudent man, wise in handling practical matters. Crown him with the knowledge necessary to be successful in all of his endeavors in life. Make him a man of insight who spares his words,

and has an excellent spirit because he is a man of under-standing.

Proverbs 13:16, 14:18, 17:27

Father, thank You that because of the inner knowledge of Your Word, my husband's chambers (his home, business, and ministry) are filled with all precious and pleasant riches. Thank You for making him a wise, strong leader and for causing his strength to increase because of his knowledge of You and Your Word.

Proverbs 24

Thank You for blessing my husband and for surrounding him like a shield with Your favor. In Your favor rests my husband's power, and in Your strength, his influence is exalted. Thank You for blessing me with a good man, one who deals graciously in his career and ministry, and lends to others. Thank You for guiding his business affairs with discretion.

Psalm 5:12, 89:17, 112:5

Chapter 20

PROVERBS PRAYERS

Proverbs is a book of wisdom for the believer. Every page of the book of Proverbs supplies us with the spiritual insight and understanding we need in order to live a righteous life. Its instructions are practical, yet life changing. Praying a proverb each day will transform your husband's life.

Proverbs 1

Father, the purpose of Proverbs is to teach my husband wisdom and discipline, and to help him understand wise sayings. I thank You that through these proverbs, my husband will receive instruction in discipline, good conduct, and doing what is right, just, and fair. These proverbs will make the simpleminded man a clever one. Thank You that my husband is a clever man.

The fear of the Lord is the beginning of knowledge. Thank You that my husband fears You.

Only fools despise wisdom and discipline. Thank You that my husband welcomes wisdom and Your discipline.

Father, thank You that my husband holds dear and regards what has been invested in him from both his natural parents and his spiritual parents. His life is crowned with grace and clothed with honor.

Lord, I pray my husband listens attentively to the words of wisdom, which come from Your Word. As a result, he lives in peace and safety; he is not afraid of harm, even though harm may be all around him.

Proverbs 2

Father, I thank You my husband cries out for insight when he searches for understanding in Your Word, just as he would search for lost money or a hidden treasure. Thank You that he walks in the fear and knowledge of You.

Lord, You grant wisdom, and from Your mouth come knowledge and understanding; give my husband a hunger for the depths of Your Word. Grant him a treasure of good sense because he is godly. Thank You for being his shield and protecting him as he walks with integrity.

Father, You guard the paths of justice, and You preserve my husband as he is faithful to You. I pray he attends to Your words, the words from Your mouth; grant him understanding in what is right, just, and fair. Give him knowledge to find the right path of action every time.

Father, as Your Word enters my husband's heart, fill him with joy. Thank You that wise planning will watch over him and understanding of Your Word will keep him safe. Save him from evil people and those who have corrupt speech. Yes, save him from the immoral, adulterous woman, the one

who has deceived so many others with her words of flattery. I declare my husband always remembers his covenant with You. Open his eyes so he will see that entering her house will cause him death. I pray he sees the end of those who have followed her, that they will never reach their God-given paths of life.

Instead, my husband will stay in the Word, be prayerful, follow You, and stay on the path of righteousness even though it is hard on his flesh. For only the upright man will dwell in the land that You have provided for us.

Proverbs 3

Father, open my husband's eyes to see that Your words will give him a long and satisfying life. Give him a strong desire to be loyal to Your Word so he will keep it as he would a valuable treasure close to his heart. I declare my husband will plant Your Word deep in his heart so Your favor will rest upon him and people will respect him, honor him, and do him great favors.

Father, I pray my husband will trust in You with all his heart and he will never depend upon his own insight and limited understanding. I pray he recognizes You in every situation because You direct and make plain the direction that he is to go.

I pray my husband remains healthy and strong as he turns his back on evil. Keep him from being impressed with his own wisdom.

Father, I pray my husband honors You with our wealth and the best of our produce, no matter what it is, because

You promised to fill our bank accounts with substance and to overflow our lives with the finest.

Bring correction to my husband when he is wrong. I pray he does not ignore You or become discouraged with himself in the process. He is Your son and You discipline those You love. Thank You for loving my husband.

Father, give my husband an unquenchable thirst for Your Word. You said You would make the person happy who finds Your wisdom and gains understanding. I pray my husband sees the benefit of finding Your Word, and the profit of wisdom that is better than silver, her wages better than gold. Your wisdom is more precious than rubies, and nothing my husband could ever desire can compare to it.

Father, thank You that as my husband finds Your Word, wisdom produces life in his right hand, riches and honor in his left. It brings him honor and respect and keeps his feet from stumbling.

Thank You that my husband need not be afraid of disaster or the destruction that comes upon the wicked because You are his security. You will keep my husband's feet from being caught in a trap. Thank You that he can lie down without fear or dread and enjoy pleasant dreams because of Your Word.

Father, I pray my husband will not withhold good from those who deserve it when it is in his power to help them. Thank You that he is a trusted man who does good to others.

I pray my husband does not envy evil individuals or mimic their ways because he is Your friend. Your blessing is on his home and all that he does.

Proverbs 4

Father, thank You that my husband will never abandon the teachings of Your Word, that his heart will hold on to them so he can live. Allow wisdom to watch over my husband and, as he feeds upon Your wisdom, let it guard him, exalt and embrace him. Your wisdom, Father, will allow my husband to live for many years. Thank You that You are guiding him on a straight path. When my husband walks, his steps will not be hindered, and when he runs, he will not stumble. Do not allow my husband to let Your Word go, because it is our life.

Father, I pray that my husband keeps from setting foot on the path of the wicked, that he will not proceed in the way of evil ones. I pray he avoids the path, and if he is already there, that he may turn away from it and pass it by.

I pray my husband pays attention to Your words and listens closely to Your sayings. Do not let him lose sight of them. I declare he keeps Your words within his heart because they are life and health to his whole body.

I pray my husband guards his heart above all else, for it is the source of life, it is where You live. Remove his peace when he uses his mouth to speak dishonestly; keep his lips from devious talk. Let my husband's eyes look forward; fix his gaze straight ahead to You. I pray he carefully considers the path for his feet, so all of his ways will be established by You. Give him grace to keep from turning to the right or to the left, but keep his feet away from the very appearance of evil.

Proverbs 5

Father, I pray my husband pays attention to Your wisdom and listens carefully to Your wise counsel so he will learn to be discreet and store up knowledge. Allow him to see that although the lips of an immoral woman are as sweet as honey, and her mouth smoother than oil, the result of sin with her is bitter poison, sharp as a double-edged sword. Give him the ability to see that her feet go down to death, that her steps lead straight to the grave, and that she does not care about the path to life. Open his eyes so he will know that she will cause him to lose his honor and she will hand over to merciless people everything that he has achieved in life.

Let my husband drink water from his own well, and share his passion and love only with me, his wife. I pray my husband allows me to be his fountain of blessing. May I be a graceful deer in his eyes. May he always be satisfied with my love and my beauty.

Lord, You clearly see what every man does, and You examine every path he takes. You know that an evil man is held captive by his own sin—they are ropes that catch and hold him. Let my husband see that he will die if he exercises a lack of self-control; he will be lost because of his uncontrolled passions.

Proverbs 6

Father, give my husband the wisdom not to cosign loans for a friend or guarantee the debt of someone else. Do not let him place himself at the mercy of another. Thank You that my husband learns from watching the ant.

Even though they have no prince or ruler to make them work, they labor hard all summer, gathering food for the winter. I pray he is not a lazy man, so poverty has no place in him.

Father, thank You that my husband stays away from the seven things You detest. Thank You that he does not have haughty eyes that look down on others while overestimating himself. Thank You that my husband speaks the truth in all things, and he is not a liar. Thank You, Lord, that my husband has mercy on the innocent; his hands are not swift to bring them down. Thank You that he does not have a heart to plot evil, and his feet do not race to do wrong. I pray, Lord, that my husband is not a false witness pouring out lies, that he is not a person who sows discord among brothers.

I pray my husband keeps Your words always in his heart and ties them around his neck. Wherever he walks, Your counsel will lead him; when he sleeps, Your words will protect him. Thank You that when he wakes up in the morning, Your words will advise him. Your commands and teachings are a lamp to light the way ahead of him. Your words are the correction; Your discipline is the way to life.

Father, I pray Your commands and teachings keep my husband from the immoral woman, from the smooth tongue of the adulterous woman. My husband will not lust for her beauty. Because of Your Word, my husband will not let her coyness seduce him. I pray You open his eyes to see that a prostitute will bring him to poverty, and sleeping with another man's wife will cost him his very life.

I pray he sees Your Word declares a man cannot scoop fire into his lap and not be burned, and a man cannot walk on hot coals and not blister his feet. I speak to his spirit, so he can see the punishment belonging to the man who sleeps with another man's wife; he will not go unpunished. Open his eyes to see that the man who commits adultery is an utter fool, for he destroys his own soul. Wounds and constant disgrace are his lot, and his shame will never be erased.

Proverbs 7

I say to wisdom, "You are my husband's sister, and I call understanding his friend." Thank You, Lord, that wisdom will keep my husband from a forbidden woman or a stranger with flattering talk.

I declare that my husband receives wisdom as he gives place to Your Word. He learns to be shrewd in areas where he is inexperienced. Your Word develops common sense within him in areas where he may be foolish.

Proverbs 8

Thank You that my husband honors Your Word because Your Word is truth. I pray my husband knows wickedness is detestable to Your lips; therefore, it should be detestable to his lips. I pray all the words of his mouth are righteous and none are crooked or perverse. I pray my husband will open his heart to accept Your Word instead of silver, and knowledge of You over pure gold, for Your Word is better than precious stones and nothing my husband desires can compare with it.

Father, I pray my husband fears You; to fear You is to hate evil. I pray he hates arrogant pride, evil conduct, and perverse speech.

Thank You that because of the Word of God in his life, my husband possesses good advice and is competent. Thank You for giving him understanding and strength.

Father, it is by Your Word that kings and rulers reign and establish just laws. Thank You that my husband loves the wisdom found in Your Word, and Your Word loves my husband. When he searches for wisdom, he finds it; with wisdom are riches and honor, lasting wealth, and righteousness for his life.

Thank You that the fruit of wisdom is better than solid gold, and its harvest better than pure silver. Thank You that my husband walks with wisdom, for wisdom is found in the way of righteousness along the paths of justice. Thank You, for wisdom is giving wealth as an inheritance to my husband and is filling his treasuries.

Father, give my husband happiness when he keeps Your ways and listens to Your instruction. When he finds Your Word, he finds life and qualifies to obtain Your favor.

Proverbs 9

Father, Your Word says to fear You is the beginning of wisdom. Thank You that my husband fears You, is increasing his knowledge of You, and is becoming a man of understanding. Help him bring joy and honor to You so that his days will be many.

For the areas in which my husband is inexperienced, help him to enter into the paths of wisdom. For the areas where my husband lacks good judgment, help him to eat the bread and drink the wine of wisdom. Help him to leave inexperience behind him and live. Give him the knowledge to pursue the way of understanding.

Help my husband to be a wise man and accept correction. Place individuals around him who will instruct and teach him so that he can learn and become wiser still. Thank You for increasing his days by Your wisdom and adding years to his life. Keep him from the enticing woman who can lead him to death and hell.

Proverbs 10

Thank You that my husband has diligent hands that bring riches to our lives. I pray that he is prudent and gathers his harvest in the summer and does not bring disgrace to You by sleeping when it is harvest time.

Let Your blessings rest on my husband's head because he is righteous and his mind is mentally sharp and quick. Make his heart wise and his life secure as he accepts Your commands and lives in integrity.

Help my husband to walk as the righteous. Make his mouth a fountain of life. Give him discerning lips and wisdom to know that hatred stirs up conflicts, but love covers all offenses.

I pray that, as my husband feeds on the Word, he becomes wise and stores up knowledge. Your Word makes him rich, and his labors lead to life. Help him to be a man who follows Your instruction, to be a man on the path to life. I pray that he is not a person who conceals hatred and has lying lips. Help him not to spread slander, as a fool would.

I pray that my husband is a man of few words because when there are many words, sin is unavoidable. Thank You that my husband is wise and can control his lips. His tongue is as pure as silver because he is righteous and his lips feed many.

Let Your blessing enrich my husband and add no sorrow to it. Let wisdom be pleasurable for him, just as shameful conduct is pleasurable for a fool. Help him to fear You. Grant him his desires. Thank You for securing him and prolonging his life in you forever. Make Your way as a stronghold for my husband, and he will never be shaken.

Proverbs 11

Open my husband's eyes so he can see that dishonest scales are an abomination to You, but accurate weights are Your delight. Keep him from pride because when pride comes, disgrace follows, but with humility comes wisdom.

I pray integrity guides him and righteousness rescues him from death and clears his path. Keep him from showing contempt for our neighbor and thereby lacking common sense. I pray my husband walks in understanding and keeps silent. Do not allow him to be a gossip that goes around revealing a secret, but grace him to be trustworthy, keeping the confidence of others.

Give my husband guidance so that he does not fall. Keep many counselors around him so there is deliverance.

I pray my husband is a kind man, who benefits from sowing righteousness, which is a true reward. Let him be a delight to You. Let his conduct be blameless.

Father, I thank You my husband's seed is forever blessed because he gives freely and yet gains more. Thank You that he is an enriched and generous person, one who gives a drink of water and receives the same. My husband will never trust in his riches, but only in You.

Proverbs 12

Father, I thank and praise You that my husband loves instruction and knowledge. He is good, therefore, he obtains favor from You. Because he is righteous, his roots are immovable. I pray he is firm in his stand for You.

Father, help me be a capable wife and a crown to my husband. Let my mouth and actions never cause him shame and become like rottenness in his bones.

Cover my husband's mind and allow his thoughts to be righteous and just. Allow the power in his speech to rescue those whom the enemy desires to ambush and destroy. Father, thank You for giving my husband great insight into Your purpose and ways. Let his desire be to please only You. Keep pride and a longing to impress others far from him, Father.

Lord, give my husband daily strength to work so that his land will have plenty of food. Keep him from being idle and chasing fantasies. I pray he sees You as the greatest provider. I pray he does not desire what evil men have. Open his eyes to see that the root of the righteous produces rich fruit.

Guard my husband from evil men and from being trapped by their rebellious speech. Give him the wisdom to sense what is evil and run toward what is good. Satisfy him

with good, while the words of his mouth and the works of his own hands reward him. Keep the way of a fool far from my husband. Do not let his way be right in his own eyes, but keep him in a place where he can listen to the counsel of the wise. I pray he will ignore an insult and thereby remain reasonable.

I pray my husband speaks the truth and declares what is right. I thank You he avoids being a false or deceitful witness. I declare my husband is a man who does not speak rashly, like a piercing sword, because his is the tongue of the wise bringing healing. Thank You that my husband's lips are truthful lips and endure forever, for a lying tongue lasts only a moment. Father, I pray my husband is one who promotes peace; therefore, he has great joy. Thank You that no disaster overcomes the righteous, so that my husband has safety in You. Lord, may You delight in my husband because he is a faithful man.

Father, I thank You my husband is wise and conceals the knowledge he has concerning others. He is unlike the fool who publicizes the secrets of others. You have given him a diligent hand so he can lead. I come against laziness in his life because it leads to forced labor.

My husband's heart is free of anxiety and is not weighed down. I pray he places Your Word in his heart so it cheers him up.

I pray my husband is a righteous man who is careful in dealing with his neighbor. Your life is in the path of the righteous; his eyes are open to see that all other paths lead to death. His heart is closed to every other path.

Proverbs 13

I declare my husband to be a wise son who hears instruction, because a mocker does not listen to rebuke.

Lord, I thank You for my husband's realization that from the words of his mouth, he will enjoy good things, and if he guards his mouth, he will protect his life.

Lord, the slacker craves, yet has nothing. I thank You my husband is diligent and will be fully satisfied. My husband loves what You love and hates what You hate. You hate lying; therefore, he hates a lying tongue. Righteousness watches over people of integrity. May my husband walk in integrity all the days of his life.

I thank You because my husband is righteous and his light shines brightly, but the lamp of the wicked is extinguished. Keep him from arrogance because it leads to nothing but strife; may he realize that those who take advice gain wisdom.

I pray my husband's wealth is not obtained by fraud because it will dwindle, but as he earns it through labor, it multiplies. He has the patience to wait for Your promises because, although delayed hope makes the heart sick, when it does come, it is a tree of life. I thank You he respects Your command and is rewarded. The wisdom in him gives instruction and is a fountain of life, turning people away from the snares of death. Grant my husband good judgment that he might win favor with both You and man. I pray he is a trustworthy courier, one who brings healing. He accepts rebuke so he is honored by You and among men.

Father, I thank You my husband walks with wise individuals, so he will become wise. Keep foolish companions away from him. Thank You for wisdom with our life resources, for You said a good man leaves an inheritance to his grandchildren, and the sinner's wealth is stored up for the righteous.

My husband disciplines our children in a godly manner. Your Word says that the one who will not use the rod of correction hates his son, but the one who loves him disciplines him diligently.

Thank You that my husband is a righteous man who eats until he is satisfied.

Proverbs 14

Father, I pray my husband lives with integrity; therefore, he fears You. Allow his lips to be filled with Your wisdom and protection.

Thank You for the abundant harvest that comes to my husband. I pray he will never be a dishonest witness who utters lies, but an honest witness who does not deceive.

Thank You that knowledge comes easy to my husband because he is perceptive as a result of Your Word. I pray he stays away from a foolish man because he will gain no knowledge from his speech.

I pray my husband is a sensible man who has wisdom to consider his way, and not the stupidity of fools, which deceives them. I declare that, in You, his tent will stand strong.

My husband will seek out the wisdom in Your Word, because there is a way that seems right to a man, but the end

is the way to death. Open the eyes of my husband's heart so he can know without a doubt the direction You have chosen for his life.

I pray my husband is a loyal man, one who is good so he gets what his deeds deserve—not an inexperienced man who believes anything, but a sensible man who watches his steps. I pray my husband is one who is cautious and turns from evil. Crown him with knowledge and let the evil bow before him because he is good. Thank You for making him happy as he shows kindness to the poor. I pray he plans well so he can find loyalty and faithfulness.

Give my husband the wisdom to profit while he works hard and controls his speech because endless talk leads only to poverty. Crown my husband with wealth through Your wisdom.

I pray my husband is a truthful witness who rescues lives, in the fear of You. Give him a strong confidence and his children a place of refuge.

I pray my husband is a patient person; one who shows great understanding. Grace controls his temper, and he does not display foolishness. Give him a tranquil heart, for it is life to his body. Do not allow him to walk in jealousy, for it is rottenness to his bones. I pray my husband is kind to the needy and honors You in his life. For You said the one who oppresses the poor insults his Maker. I pray wisdom resides in the heart of my husband and makes him discerning. He is a wise servant and one favored by those in authority; I pray he is never among those who experience Your wrath.

Proverbs 15

ather, I pray my husband remembers a gentle answer turns away anger, but a harsh word stirs up wrath. I pray he knows that the tongue of the wise makes knowledge attractive, but the mouth of fools blurts out foolishness. Never let him forget that Your eyes are everywhere, observing the wicked and the good. Let his tongue be one that heals like a tree of life, and not the tongue that breaks a person's spirit.

I pray my husband does not despise his Father's instruction, but he is a person who heeds correction and is sensible.

Our house is the house of the righteous and therefore has great wealth. I pray my husband sees that trouble accompanies the income of the wicked.

Make my husband's lips the lips of the wise that broadcast knowledge; may he know that his prayer is Your delight.

Father, I pray my husband will pursue righteousness for all the days of his life. His heart is opened before You. I pray he has a joyful heart and a cheerful face, because sorrow produces a broken spirit.

Give my husband a discerning mind so that he may seek Your knowledge. May his heart be cheerful and may he continually feast upon Your Word. Father, let my husband fear You and walk in Your love. Keep a hot temper far from him and speak to his heart so he never stirs up conflict. I pray he is slow to anger and therefore calms strife.

Thank You, Lord, for making my husband diligent and not a slacker whose way is like a thorny hedge. My husband's path is a highway.

Lord, I pray my husband brings joy to his father. Keep foolish things away from him and never let him despise his mother. I thank You he is a man with understanding who walks a straight path.

I pray my husband's plans do not fail, because he has great counsel. Thank You for surrounding him with many advisers. His plans will succeed.

My husband is a man who takes joy in giving an answer; let his words be timely and good to the hearer.

Because he feeds on Your Word, my husband is a discerning man whose path of life leads upward, away from depths of hell. Keep pride far from my husband because You destroy the house of the proud. Your fear is wisdom's instruction, and humility comes before honor.

My husband will not have plans that are detestable to You. Let his words be pleasant and pure. My husband will not be one who profits dishonestly because he knows it would make trouble for our household. I pray he is one who hates bribery so that he will live. My husband has the mind of the righteous, because a righteous person thinks before answering. He is not one who blurts out evil things with his mouth.

I pray Your ears are opened to my husband because he is a righteous man, and You are far from the wicked. My husband's eyes are bright with Your Word. You Word cheers his heart. He allows the good news of Your Word to strengthen

his bones. I pray he has an ear that listens to life-giving rebuke so he is at home among the wise. My husband is not one who ignores instruction, therefore despising himself. May my husband listen to correction so he can acquire good sense.

Proverbs 16

Father, as my husband's heart reflects the things he desires, I pray he will come to You for the answer so he can know which way he is to go. I pray his motives are always in line with Your will. Do not allow his ways to seem right in his own eyes if they do not measure up with Your Word and direction for his life. My husband will commit his activities to You, Lord, so his plans will be accomplished. I pray my husband knows You have prepared everything in his life for Your purpose—even the unbeliever who may bring trouble to his days. Keep his heart right, because a proud heart is detestable to You and will not go unpunished. Lord, I pray my husband's ways please you so You will make his enemies walk in peace with him. As my husband plans his way, Father, continue to determine and direct his steps.

My husband has balance in his life and understands it is better to have little with righteousness than a great income with injustice. Because You carry his weight, my husband knows not to worry. He walks in honesty and integrity, and You will fulfill Your plan for his life.

Keep wicked behavior far from my husband because it is detestable to great leaders. Righteousness will engulf every fiber of his being so he can stand with those in leadership.

My husband has righteous lips because they are a king's delight. My husband walks in absolute honesty. He has the wisdom to appease the anger of his leader, and the ability to discern when favor and life is present with the leader.

My husband has Your wisdom because it is better than gold! He has understanding because it is preferable to silver. I pray my husband avoids evil. Guard his way so he can protect his life. Keep pride, which comes before destruction, and an arrogant spirit, which comes before a fall—far from my husband. He sees that it really is better to be lowly of spirit with the humble than to divide spoils with the proud. Lord, I thank You my husband has understanding in all matters so he can find success. He trusts in You and lives a happy life. Thank You, Lord, for making my husband one with a wise heart so he is called discerning. My husband increases his learning with the pleasant speech You have given him.

I pray my husband possesses insight so it will be a fountain of life for him. Wisdom instructs his mouth and learning increases his speech. Father, I thank You his words are pleasant as a honeycomb, sweet to the taste. They are health and healing to his body. His eyes are open so he is not tempted to go the way that seems right, but leads to death.

My husband has an appetite for You so he will work for You. His hunger urges him on in the ways of God. He does not dig up evil in his life or anyone else's, nor is his speech like a scorching fire. I thank You my husband does not sow strife or separate friendships with gossip. My husband sees and discerns those around him. His eyes are open to see the violent man who lures his neighbor, leading him in a way that is not good. He will recognize the one who devises perverse things and brings about evil.

As my husband ages, he knows his gray hair is a glorious crown; it is found in the way of righteousness. He will never despise his age or go through a mid-life crisis.

Lord, my husband is a man of patience because patience is better than power, and controlling one's temper is better than capturing a city.

Proverbs 17

Father, I pray my husband is a man of peace and he keeps our home free of strife. He is a wise servant and rules over and above others. He shares in the inheritance You have given to Your sons.

Father, try my husband's heart. I declare he keeps away from the wicked person who listens to or initiates malicious talk. He runs from the liar who pays attention to a person with a destructive tongue. Father, I pray my husband will never mock the poor and insult You. He will not rejoice over calamity, even if it is toward his enemy, because it leads to punishment.

My husband loves our children. His sons and daughters are his pride and his grandchildren his crown.

I pray my husband does not yield his mouth to excessive speech or lies. Lord, my husband conceals an offense and promotes Your love. He does not gossip about the matter and separate friends. Father, I pray my husband is a perceptive person and adheres to rebuke. He keeps away from a foolish man in his foolishness. He knows not to return evil for good

and cause evil to dwell permanently in our home. I pray my husband is not one who starts a conflict and releases a flood of strife; instead he stops disputes before they break out. My husband is a friend who loves at all times, and is a brother who is born for difficult times in the lives of others.

Lord, my husband's mind is focused on You because a man with a twisted mind will not succeed and a man with deceitful speech will fall into ruin.

Father, I thank You my husband's heart is joyful for it is good medicine; a broken spirit will dry up his bones.

My husband avoids being influenced by the wicked man and is not a man who secretly takes a bribe to subvert the course of justice. He has wisdom for it is the focus of the perceptive; a fool's eyes roam to the ends of the earth. My husband is not a foolish son who gives grief to his father or bitterness to the one who bore him.

Give my husband wisdom so that he will not punish an innocent person, or beat a noble person for their honesty. Do not allow my husband to show partiality to the guilty by perverting the justice due the innocent.

My husband has intelligence to restrain his words; he keeps a cool head so he is a man of understanding. He is wise when he keeps silent, and discerning when he seals his lips.

Proverbs 18

Lord, my husband is not one who isolates himself and pursues selfish desires. He does not rebel against wise judgment. He delights in understanding and does not desire to show off his opinions.

140

My husband sees that when a wicked man comes, shame follows, along with dishonor and disgrace.

Thank You that the words of my husband's mouth are deep waters, a flowing river, and a fountain of wisdom. My husband will not have a fool's lips, which lead to strife, or a mouth that provokes violence, because a fool's mouth is his devastation and his lips are a trap. My husband has no desire to gossip, for a gossip's words are like choice food that goes down to a person's innermost being.

My husband has strength so he is not one who is truly lazy in his work, because You said a lazy worker is *"brother to him who is a great destroyer"* (v. 9).

I thank You, Lord, for Your name is a strong tower. My husband can run to it and is safe.

My husband knows a rich man's wealth is his fortified city, his self-esteem is like a high wall. My husband will only depend on You and never on money.

My husband does not keep a prideful heart because it will produce his downfall. His eyes are open so he knows that before honor comes humility.

I pray my husband is not a man who gives an answer before he listens, for this is foolishness and shame for him.

You have given my husband's spirit the grace to endure sickness. Please guard my husband from a broken spirit. Thank You my husband has the mind of the discerning and the ear of the wise so he can seek and acquire knowledge. I pray my husband's gifts open doors for him and bring him before great men.

My husband is not easily offended, for an offended brother is harder to reach than a fortified city, and their quarrels are like the bars of a fortress.

My husband's mouth is filled with good things because Your Word states, from the fruit of his mouth, a man's stomach is satisfied. My husband's life is filled with the product of his lips. He will always remember life and death are in the power of his tongue, and those who love it will eat its fruit.

Thank You my husband is a man who has found a wife, and thus, found a good thing. Thank You for the favor that comes from You.

My husband has many friends because he himself is friendly. But he knows that You stick to him closer than a brother.

Proverbs 19

Lord, I thank You my husband is a man who walks in integrity. He is not a man who has foolish, deceitful lips. Zeal that comes without knowledge is not a part of my husband's life. He does not act hastily and sin. His own foolishness will not lead him astray so that his heart will rage and blame You.

When my husband enters into his place of wealth, he will have the wisdom to know who his friends really are. My husband is not a false witness nor is he one who utters lies. Thank You for the favor You have given my husband with his leaders, spiritual and secular.

My husband is in a place where he acquires good sense because it shows he loves his own soul. Let him be one who

safeguards understanding and finds good things. My husband's insight gives him patience, and his virtue overlooks an offense. He is quick to forgive. I pray that even among the most evil of bosses, my husband finds favor, and it is like dew on the grass.

Lord, I thank You I am not a wife whose nagging is as an endless dripping. My husband receives his home and wealth as an inheritance from his father, but I am a sensible wife who has been sent by You, Lord.

My husband is not lazy or one who sleeps excessively. He is not like the idle who will go hungry. My husband is a man who follows orders; he is one who keeps commands and preserves his soul. He will not be one who disregards Your ways and dies.

Lord, I thank You my husband displays kindness to the poor because, in doing so, he is lending to You, and Your Word declares that You will pay wonderful interest on his loan.

My husband has the wisdom to discipline our children while there is hope. He will never become so angry that he has thoughts of abusing them because Your Word says a person with great anger bears the penalty. If such a man is rescued, he will just have to be rescued again.

My husband will listen closely to counsel and receive instruction so he may be wise later in life. Many plans are in my husband's heart, but, Lord, I thank You that Your decree will prevail in his life. My husband is a man whose desire is to be kind; he will not live his life as a lie or a hypocrite. My husband fears You and that fear leads to life; because he fears You, he can sleep at night without fear of danger.

My husband is not a slacker who buries his hand in the bowl and does not even bring it back to his mouth. He is one who is willing to learn. Give him a teachable spirit; if he is a mocker, correct him, and he will learn a lesson if he needs to be corrected. Rebuke him so he will gain knowledge. My husband will respect, forgive, and love his parents, for You said the one who mistreats his father and chases away his mother is a disgraceful and shameful son. My husband will not stop listening to instruction and stray from the words of knowledge.

Proverbs 20

*M*y husband will keep from wine, for he knows it is a mocker. He stays away from alcohol because it is a brawler. Whoever is led astray by them is not wise.

Father, thank You for the wisdom You have given my husband to confront an angry leader. He knows to resolve disputes using Your Word and does not get himself into quarrels.

My husband is not like the lazy man who fails to plow and, at harvest time, must beg because he has nothing. I thank You that Your counsel in my husband's heart is like deep water; he is a man of understanding who knows how to draw it out. My husband is not a man who proclaims his own loyalty, but is a faithful, trustworthy man. My husband is the one who lives with integrity and is righteous; our children who come after him will be blessed.

Father, my husband is a leader who is positioned to judge righteously. He scatters all evil with his eyes. I declare my

husband will confidently say, "I have made my heart pure; I am pure from my sin." The actions in his life are not detestable to You; they reveal his behavior is pure and right. My husband has a hearing ear and seeing eyes because You made them both. He hears those things that build and edify him in You; he will not permit his eyes to view anything that does not please You.

I thank You, Father, for my husband does not love to sleep and will not become poor; his eyes are open, so he will always have enough to eat.

Deception is not in my husband; he does not deceive other people or operate in business deceitfully.

I declare my husband knows that the lips of knowledge are a rare treasure, as gold and a multitude of jewels.

My husband will never obtain food deceitfully, for it starts out sweet but afterward his mouth will seem full of gravel.

My husband finalizes his God-given plans through counsel and fights his battles with sound guidance.

I declare my husband is not one who reveals secrets as a constant gossip; and he avoids those with big mouths.

My husband will never curse his father or mother, because Your Word says this individual's lamp will be put out in deep darkness.

Father, I thank You my husband's success will be steady and sure because an inheritance gained hastily will not be blessed in the end.

My husband will not take revenge on his own; he will wait on You, Lord, and You will save him.

Today I pray that my husband will always deal with an even hand, never under the table, deceiving or lying to others. Open his eyes so he can see his steps are determined by You. Draw him into Your presence so he can gain the insight his heart so desires. Show him that he cannot understand his own way without You.

My husband will not be trapped by devoting or committing himself to something unholy. Give him wisdom to consider his vows before he ever makes them. As a leader, he separates wicked from good and removes evil from his presence. His spirit is Your lamp, and You search the innermost parts of his heart. Father, seek out those things that only You can see.

Thank You that my husband is merciful and truthful, for these qualities will always deliver him as a leader. Through loyalty, he will maintain his place of authority. His glory as a young man is his strength; his splendor when he is old is his gray hair.

The lashes and wounds my husband has experienced purge away evil, and discipline cleanses his innermost parts.

Proverbs 21

Father, thank You my husband's heart is a river of water in Your hand; direct it wherever You choose. Evaluate his motives and keep him from living his life in a way that is right in his own eyes. Help him submit his thoughts concerning his life and the life of our family to You. When he does right, it is more acceptable to You than sacrifice.

I decree that my husband does not walk with haughty eyes or a proud heart because it is sin and the lamp that guides the wicked man. He is a diligent man, and his plans will lead to profit. Do not allow him to become a reckless or poor man.

Keep my husband sensitive to Your presence in his life and keep his lips from lying. He is a just man, and his conduct is not wicked, but innocent and upright. He is taught by wise men; he acquires knowledge that will help his business and ministry grow. He is an example of a righteous man; he considers the house of the wicked and will overthrow it by leading those within it to Jesus Christ.

Thank You for opening my husband's ears to the cries of the poor; he will always remember them in his giving. My husband will not be like the man who wanders from the way of wisdom, because his life is before You. Help him crucify his flesh so he does not love pleasure, wine, and oil more than You and end up a poor man.

The wicked are before my husband because they are a ransom for him, and the unfaithful person is harvest for the upright. Thank You that precious treasure and oil are in the dwelling of my husband. He is not like a foolish man who squanders all that You have given him. He pursues righteousness and mercy, and finds life, righteousness, and honor in You. Guard his life when others compromise their walk with You.

I decree that my husband is a man of holiness in all he says and does. Keep what is vital before him, and place within his heart a hunger for only You. My husband is wise because he wins souls. He is equipped to win our city for You

and able to bring down the devil's mightiest strongholds in peoples' lives.

Thank You that my husband guards his mouth and tongue and keeps himself out of trouble. Pride and arrogance flee from his life, and he submits himself to You. He is not like the lazy man whose desires lead to destruction because his hands refuse to work. My husband is righteous; he is generous and does not hold back. Grant him to know the sacrifice of a wicked person is detestable—and even more so when he brings it with wicked intent! May my husband be a man who listens and then speaks successfully, because Your Word says a liar will perish.

Thank You for the wisdom that allows my husband to see past the bold faces of the wicked and allow him to consider the ways of the wicked. Keep deception far from him. On my husband's best day he realizes he will always need You and his deliverance comes only from You.

Proverbs 22

Father, thank You my husband desires a good name over great wealth, and Your favor more than silver and gold. Thank You for making him a great man. Give him the ability he needs to foresee evil wherever it might be and help him take cover in You. Thank You he will not move forward in the face of danger. He walks in humility and fears You, and it brings with it wealth, honor, and life. Help him to guard himself and stay away from the thorns and snares on the path of the perverse.

I praise You that the godly things invested in my husband when he was young will guide, direct, and keep him

148

as he continues in life. Give him wisdom to live a debt-free life, for You said the rich will rule over the poor, and the borrower will be a slave to the lender. Position him to pay off all our debts: our house, our car, credit cards and any other outstanding debt that we may have.

My husband will never be a man who sows injustice and reaps sorrow. The rod of his anger will not destroy him. He is a generous man, one who shares what he has with those less fortunate. He is a peaceful man, who draws others to You. He will never be a mocker or one who brings conflict wherever he goes. He surrounds himself with individuals who have pure hearts and words of grace, and he lives in the favor of those with influence.

I declare the knowledge of Your Word is deep in my husband's heart, and Your eyes keep watch over that knowledge and it produces results in his life. He will not give heed to the mouth of the forbidden woman who is like a deep pit. Many men have fallen into her trap, but I decree my husband will not. Thank You for keeping him before Your face, Father.

Thank You for giving my husband wisdom in using the rod of discipline to drive foolishness from the hearts of our children.

I pray my husband never gives to the rich while oppressing the poor in order to enrich himself, for it will surely lead to poverty. Give him the strength to listen closely, and pay attention to words of wisdom; help him to apply his heart to his knowledge of You. Your Word is pleasing to my husband if he keeps it within him and fixes it on his lips. Your Word instructs my husband, and his confidence becomes strong

in You. Speak to him about counsel and knowledge in all he does, so he can learn true and reliable words and give a trustworthy report to those in authority.

My husband will not make friends with angry or hot-tempered men. For if he does, he will learn their ways and entangle himself in a snare. He will not be one who enters agreements to put up security for loans. Give my husband wisdom when making financial decisions, which might affect our family now and in generations to come. Help him place value on what those before him have built and worked hard to provide.

Thank You for giving my husband skills and abilities that will place him in the presence of influential and well-known men.

Proverbs 23

Father, I thank You that You have given my husband wisdom to consider what he is doing at all times and he will not desire the food of the wicked. Help him not to wear himself out to get rich. Illuminate his heart to know that when he fixes his eyes on riches, they disappear and take flight.

My husband is sensitive and knows those around him. Keep him from desiring the food of a stingy man, for such a man thinks of nothing but cost. Keep my husband from wasting his time or his words. He will give his words of wisdom to those who will not despise them like fools. He has the knowledge and understanding to know where and when to purchase land. He will not take advantage of the poor or fatherless, because You are their Redeemer and will take their side. My husband applies himself to the instruction found in Your words, and listens to Your words of knowledge.

Lord, my husband has been given the responsibility of training our children. Help him not to withhold correction when they need it. Give him wisdom in applying the rod of discipline. Thank You that when he disciplines them, he is rescuing their lives from hell. Your wisdom is necessary to raise our children. He will invest solid wisdom in their lives so our hearts can rejoice and we can make You glad, Father. Help us to train our children to use their mouths to speak what is right.

Do not allow my husband to envy the wicked when they prosper, but let him fear You all his days. He has a future and a hope that is eternal in You. Thank You he is a man who listens and becomes wise; he keeps his mind and his heart on the right course. Thank You he does not associate with those who drink too much or gorge themselves, satisfying their flesh, because Your Word says the drunkard and the glutton will become poor, and drowsiness will clothe such a man in rags.

I declare my husband to be a faithful man. He is not the man who will be drawn in by a seductive woman. For such a woman is a deep pit, a narrow well, who sets a trap of temptation and aims to increase the number of unfaithful men.

Thank You my husband stays away from alcohol, which only increases sorrow, arguments, complaints, and insults. He does not gaze or desire it. He knows that although it goes

down smooth, in the end it bites like a serpent and stings like a viper. Thank You that he does not drink and see or say strange and perverse things.

Proverbs 24

L et my husband not desire to be in the company of evil men, for their hearts devise violence and their talk stirs up trouble.

My husband is able to build up our home with his wisdom and establish it by his understanding. By the knowledge of Your Word, the rooms for our life are filled with precious and beautiful treasures. Thank You that my husband has strength that comes from wisdom and undertakes every situation with sound guidance and victory because he listens to a multitude of wise counselors.

Thank You for giving my husband Your wisdom, which is far too lofty for a fool. Thank You for filling him, and those around him, with words from above. Keep scheming far from him because it is evil.

Lord, my husband gains inner strength as he seeks You through prayer and Your Word. When difficult times come, his strength is not limited. Thank You he is able to help others; You have given him wisdom and strength to rescue those being led astray, and to save those stumbling toward eternal destruction. Thank You that my husband has a heart to reach the lost for You.

As sweet as honey is to the taste, wisdom is to my husband. He has found it and has a future; his hope will never be cut off. When the wicked set an ambush for my husband, though he may fall, seven times he will get up again. My husband will keep his heart in the right place and never rejoice when his enemy falls or stumbles, because he wants to please You.

My husband does not worry about the actions of evildoers, nor does he envy the wicked, because they have no future and their lamp will be put out. My husband fears You and those who lead him. He does not associate with rebellious people because their destruction will come suddenly. Thank You that he is able to judge situations fairly. Help him to judge between the innocent and the guilty, so that a generous blessing will come to him. He will always give an honest answer.

Thank You that my husband is prepared for the work you have given him, and he keeps his priorities in the right place. He walks in love and forgiveness. He never lies about anyone or deceives with his lips; he does not seek revenge, but allows Your vengeance. My husband does not reside in laziness, or fall into the trap of the lazy man and come to ruin.

Proverbs 25

Father, my husband has the understanding and the desire to draw out the matters that You have concealed. Remove wicked men from his presence. Let the throne of his life, his business and ministry, be established in righteousness.

Thank You that my husband is not a bragger especially before his leaders and that promotion comes to his life because he has humbled himself. If he has a dispute with an

individual, he will resolve the issue without going to court and revealing the person's problem. He will not be disgraced in public.

Father, I thank You for giving my husband wisdom—wisdom to speak words at the right time and offer correction to receptive ears. He is Your trustworthy messenger, one who brings You joy. He is not the man who boasts about a gift that he has not given. He is a man of faith that speaks what he has positioned himself to receive. My husband has favor with his boss and leadership, and You have given him patience and a gentle tongue. He does all things in moderation so he will not overwork himself and become sick.

My husband will not overstay his welcome in the home of our friends or neighbors. He does not place his confidence in an unfaithful person in a time of trouble. He walks in the love of God and blesses his enemy. If his enemy is thirsty, my husband gives him something to drink; if he is hungry, my husband will feed him. My husband will repay harm with kindness. Thank You that my husband does not gossip and his tongue does not cause anger. He is a righteous man; he does not yield to the wicked, lose his temper, or seek after his own glory.

Proverbs 26

Father, as a righteous man, my husband is worthy of the honor You have given him. Thank You, because he lives his life in a way that keeps away curses. He avoids the foolish who have no concept of Your ways. Thanks to Your understanding and wisdom, he will not hire them or trust them. My husband is not wise in his own eyes, but he

trust in You. You have already given him the endurance he needs so he will not become lazy and fail to finish the course You have directed for him.

Thank You because my husband minds his own business and stays out of the quarrels of others. Deception, conflict, gossip, and a lying tongue are far from him. He works hard to keep his heart pure before You. Your Spirit of love makes it hard for him to harbor bitterness or hatred in his heart. He speaks words of encouragement with the right heart, not a heart filled with evil.

Proverbs 27

I decree my husband does not boast about tomorrow, for he does not know what a day might bring. Others may praise my husband, but it will not come from his own mouth. He does not walk in jealously. He understands that an open rebuke is better than concealed love. He knows that the wounds of a friend are faithful, but the kisses of an enemy are a lie. My husband is a valuable friend and remains true, even in tough times. Thank You because he is a good friend who has good friends.

Lord, thank You for giving my husband a heart that appreciates all You accomplish in our lives; he does not take Your many blessings for granted. He finds joy in our home; he does not wander like a bird from its nest. I am glad that his life brings You great joy. He is a sensible man who can foresee danger and take cover, for the foolish keep going and are punished.

Lord, there is a place in the life of my husband for his friends; he understands their place in his life. He will not

sacrifice his relationship with his wife or children for the sake of his friends. He has Your knowledge concerning his friends so he will always know how to answer them and to move in and out among them. Thank You that he is one who mentors and invests in other men, because as iron sharpens iron, so one man sharpens another.

Father, in the times when it seems that I am nagging or driving him away, thank You that my husband has Your wisdom and that he walks in the Spirit and not in his flesh.

My husband serves his leader faithfully, and one day he will be honored. As water reflects the face, so does my husband's heart reflects the kind of man he is. My husband's eyes view things that help him develop his life in You. His inner peace leaves if he sees things he should not see. His satisfaction comes from viewing the Word of God.

The praises that my husband receives test him and determine where his heart is. He glories in Your praises and not those from men. Thank You for wisdom and knowledge concerning the management of our bank accounts and our financial portfolio; he pays close attention to what You have blessed us with because wealth is not forever. You have given him Your insight to be a faithful steward of what You have given him.

Proverbs 28

Father, in the name of Jesus, thank You that my husband is righteous and as bold as a lion; he is a discerning and knowledgeable ruler, therefore his company

will endure. He is not a destitute leader who oppresses the poor. He does not reject the laws of God or man and therefore understands all things.

My husband lives a life of integrity; he keeps your law; he is kind to the poor, and will not receive wealth as one who collects excessive interest. He never turns his ear away from hearing Your law, and his prayer is Your delight. He walks blamelessly and inherits good things. He does not lead the upright into evil ways. My husband is a rich man, yet he is not wise in his own eyes; he has a powerful sense of discernment. He is righteous and will therefore triumph in all things. He does not conceal his sins so that he does not prosper, but he confesses and forsakes his sins and finds mercy in You.

My husband is happy because he is always reverent toward You and Your Word. He never hardens his heart and falls into trouble. He is quick to understand and he will not oppress others. He is one who hates covetousness and prolongs his life. My husband will never be a man burdened by bloodshed or guilt and he is not a fugitive. He lives with integrity and is helped by You. He will not distort right and wrong, or enter into perversity, which will cause a sudden fall.

Father, thank You my husband works with his hands and we always have plenty of food. He never positions himself to chase frivolity and, therefore, invite poverty. You have revealed to my husband that faithful men have many blessings, but one in a hurry to get rich will be punished. My husband does not compromise, show partiality, or sin for a piece of bread. He is not an evil man in a hurry for

wealth; he understands poverty will come to such an individual.

My husband rebukes a person and finds more favor than one who flatters with his tongue. My husband will not rob from his father or his mother, but he prospers by the works of his own hands. My husband always trusts in You and therefore prospers. He is not a greedy person who provokes conflict. He does not trust in himself because You said the one who trusts in himself is a fool, but whoever walks in wisdom will be saved. Thank You my husband walks in Your wisdom and is protected.

Father, it is on my husband's heart continually to give to the poor so we will never be in need. He will not turn his eyes away from the poor and receive many curses.

Proverbs 29

Father, I thank You my husband does not harden his neck when he is rebuked, for such men will be destroyed without remedy. He is righteous, and in authority; he loves wisdom and his father rejoices. He rejects the companion of harlots, which seek to destroy his wealth. My husband establishes justice in the land. He refrains from flattering his neighbor, therefore preventing traps set for him. He is a righteous man; therefore, transgression finds him singing and rejoicing. My husband considers the cause of the poor; he is wise and turns away wrath. He does not pay attention to lies, which cause his entire house to become wicked.

Thank You that my husband judges the poor with truth, establishing his throne forever. He raises our children with

spiritual insight as he brings discipline and correction. When wickedness and rebellion increase, my righteous husband can see its downfall. He brings correction to our son who, in turn, gives delight to our soul.

Father, my husband remains self-controlled because You have given him a vision for his life. He is happy to follow Your commands. He is slow to speak as not to be among fools; he rejects the actions of angry men, which cause conflict and rebellion. My husband is humble in spirit and retains his honor; he is safe because he trusts in You.

I praise You because my husband understands that justice comes from You. He is upright in all his ways.

Proverbs 30

Thank You that my husband is an intelligent man, one who has the ability to understand. He has gained wisdom and has knowledge of You, the Holy One. Every word from You is pure. You are a shield to my husband because he has put his trust in You. He does not add to Your words, therefore he is not rebuked or found to be a liar. He keeps falsehood and deceitful words far from him. Whether he is in riches or in poverty, my husband is content for You have provided for him and met his every need. He will not become so full with life and things that he denies You.

You have given my husband the understanding he needs, and he does not slander a fellow employee to his employer; he is not a troublemaker. He honors, blesses, and respects his father and his mother; he does not curse them. My husband is not wise in his own eyes, and You have washed him from

159

his former lifestyle. My husband is a part of the generation that honors You, Lord God.

Father, in a world that is never satisfied, thank You that my husband finds satisfaction in You and in Your Word. Father, I thank You that my husband finds peace and understanding in Your Word. When he has done wrong, he does not cover or hide his sin but is quick to confess them to you. Like the ant, my husband works hard and does what is necessary in order to provide a comfortable home for our family. Pride is far from him; he casts down evil thoughts, is slow to speak, and walks in the love of God, avoiding strife at all cost.

Proverbs 31

Thank You that my husband is a leader and therefore realizes that neither wine nor beer is for him to desire because they will cause him to forget what You decree.

Thank You that my husband will speak up for those who have no voice, for the justice of all who are dispossessed. Give him the wisdom and courage to speak up, judge righteously, and defend the cause of the oppressed and needy.

Chapter 21

A VIRTUOUS WOMAN'S CONFESSION: PROVERBS 31

*The book of Proverbs ends with a list of qualities
for a godly woman. For thousands of years,
God-fearing women have looked to the noble, or
virtuous, woman of Proverbs 31 as their ideal.
Traditionally, this "poem" was recited in Jewish
homes on the eve of the Sabbath. I can imagine a
young Mary, the future mother of Jesus, holding
this image before her as an example. Two
thousand years later, this is still God's idea of a
virtuous woman. Let this be our prayer for the
type of woman we desire to be within our homes.*

Father, I thank You that my husband does not spend his energy on strange women or his efforts on those who destroy kings.

I am a virtuous woman, more precious than jewels and the heart of my husband trusts in me.

My husband does not lack anything good because I reward him with good, not evil, all the days of my life.

I select the best and work with willing hands; I am like the merchant ships, bringing needed provision.

I arise while it is still night and provide food for our household, and portions for those who help us.

I evaluate good investments and move wisely as I am led, bringing continual increase into our household.

I draw upon my inner strength; my arms are strong in the Lord.

I can see that the fruit of my work is good, and my lamp never goes out at night because I always work to produce more in our lives.

I am not afraid of hard work and I extend my hands to the poor and the needy.

I am not afraid when the seasons of our life change, because everyone in my household has their need meet.

I am creative and wise, and wear the finest of clothing.

My husband has a good reputation within the city, in the places where he sits, and among the leaders of the land.

I am strong in business and produce powerful results because strength and honor are my clothing. I am optimistic about the future.

My mouth opens with wisdom, and loving instruction is on my tongue.

I watch over the activities of our household and I am never idle.

My children rise up and call me blessed, and my husband praises me.

Many women are capable, but I surpass them all!

Charm is deceptive and beauty is fleeting, but I am a woman who fears the Lord, and I am praised.

I receive the reward of my labor, and my life is respected throughout the city.

Chapter 22

OTHER PRAYERS FOR HUSBANDS

Below are prayers that a few of my friends have prayed for their husbands. They are prayers that can be prayed daily, or as they are needed. Many of these women have experienced life situations that may be similar to your own. Please allow the Holy Spirit to minister to you as you pray them.

For the husband needing strength to lead his family

Father, in the name of Jesus, I thank You that my husband is a visionary. He listens to Your voice and receives direction to lead our family into fulfilling Your purpose. He is the priest and prophet in our home. He comes before You on behalf of our household, just as Aaron and Moses came to You on behalf of the people of Israel.

He speaks into my life divine utterances from Your Word and it is prophecy. Just like You, he calls those things that are not as though they are. Thank You for ordering his steps in Your Word and establishing his ways upon Your principles.

Lord, my husband's delight is in You. Thank You for giving him a hunger to meditate on Your Word, day and night. He is planted like a tree by the rivers of waters. Our home is planted, our lives are planted, and our children are planted in the depths of You.

Father, I praise You because I know that Your peace follows him, and Your anointing rests on him. Everything he does will prosper. He hides Your Word in his heart and does not sin against You. Your Word is his daily guide.

Strengthen me to minister to my husband so his desires will never turn toward another. He will make a covenant with his eyes and will not look at another woman to lust after her, thereby committing adultery in his heart. He avoids youthful lust, and a strange woman will not ensnare him.

Thank You that my husband submits himself to You so he can resist the devil and put him to flight in his life. My husband loves me as Christ loves the church; he is willing to give up his life for our sake.

Thank You that my husband ministers to me as the weaker vessel, and I minister to him, as he is the head of our marriage. Thank You for my husband's knowledge and wisdom; may he use them to increase Your kingdom in this natural realm.

My husband has the ability to sow our seed, and possesses the wisdom not to consume it. He plants in good soil, and it yields great increase in our lives, and positions us to bless others. My husband's faith increases as he attends to the Word, and he lives his life with expectancy. He believes

strongly for a supernatural return on every seed we have ever sown, both spiritually and materially.

Thank You for giving me the grace to submit to my husband's leadership as he humbles himself and submits himself to You. My desire is to build him up, because I am the helper You fashioned me to be before the foundation of the world. Help me regard my husband as leader, just as Sarah regarded Abraham as lord, understanding this represents his God-given place of authority in our lives.

Thank You because I am a wise woman who builds her home. Teach me to live the life of the Proverbs 31 woman so nothing is lacking as I minister to my husband. I accept the wisdom to keep You first while balancing my life, our family, home, career, and ministry.

For the believing husband

Heavenly Father, thank You, Lord, for my husband and for the ministry You placed in him. You have filled him with the Holy Spirit and covered him with the blood of Jesus. God, I thank You for encamping angels all about him, and for Your omnipresence in every activity of his life.

Before You formed my husband in the womb, You knew him and predestined him for greatness. He does not allow anyone to look down on him because of his youth, but sets an example for others in speech, life, love, faith, and purity.

Thank You he will not cast away his confidence, because it has great recompense of reward. I thank You that my husband has the mind of Christ, and because he is a good man, every step he takes is ordered in Your Word.

You placed within him great wisdom, just as Solomon. He leads our family, and the gifts of the Spirit are rich within him. Thank You for covering my husband from dangers seen and unseen. And, though the weapons of the enemy may form against him, they shall not prosper. My husband is Your righteousness, made perfect in Your image.

Thank You for planting my husband like a tree beside the rivers of flowing water. He is rooted and grounded in Your Word, which is the foundation of his life. Thank You for giving him Your favor; it rests heavy on his life and Your grace abounds richly toward him.

I declare that my husband is a giver, and with the same measure he gives, it will be given back unto him.

Thank You for knowing the thoughts You think towards him—thoughts of peace, and not of evil, in order to bring him to an expected end.

Father, Your joy is his strength; Your Word is a lamp unto his feet and a light unto his path. He will not get weary in doing good, but will reap because he does not grow faint. Because of Your mercies, he is not consumed. Thank You that Your compassions do not fail him.

Thank You for strengthening me to be available to my husband in order to meet His needs, and for binding us together in love. Thank You he can build himself on his most holy faith by praying in the Spirit. Because You have poured Your love into my husband, he loves me as You love the church. As an act of my will, I submit to my husband and reciprocate Your perfect love toward him.

You have blessed my husband to be a good father; he teaches my children the way they should live and they do not depart from it. He seeks first Your kingdom and its righteousness, and You add all things to his life. You have already supplied every need that we will ever have. Help him to draw on that provision in our lives.

You made my husband the salt of the earth, and he is Your righteousness. His life honors You; men see his good works and give You glory. Thank You for granting him strength like Samson, wisdom like Solomon, and the spirit of a servant like Timothy. You are greater in my husband than the enemy who lives in the world.

For the unbelieving husband

Father, in the name of Jesus, thank You so much for my husband. He is the head of this house and he submits himself to You as his head. Thank You for covering him and anointing him from the top of his head to the soles of his feet. You have dispatched angels around him all day long, and no hurt, harm, or danger will come to him.

Father, I thank You that I am my husband's gift from You. I love him and he loves me. The love we have for each other is Your love. Help us to remember it is unconditional, it is faithful, and it is loyal.

You have given him a peace, which surpasses all understanding, and there is no room for the spirit of confusion in his life. Thank You, Father, because You are his peace. His heart is after Your own. Continue to touch his heart and his mind, may his desires be to please only You.

Thank You for directing his every step and decision. I pray my husband will be a born again, Spirit-filled man, one who runs away from evil. May his life burn for you. Your salvation belongs to our entire household. Thank You that this includes my husband. When You gave Your plan of salvation, You had my husband in mind.

I praise You for the ability to stand firm on Your Word. It produces life in abundance, to the full, until it overflows. Because I trust in You, there is nothing impossible, and my husband's destiny is found only in You. You will never leave him nor forsake him. Every promise You have made will come to pass in his life. I speak life into his life, and I know that You have ordained him to serve You before the foundation of the world. I declare that my husband is saved, my husband is delivered, my husband is set free. May he use the days of his life to build Your kingdom.

Thank You so much, Father, for hearing my prayer as You always do. I give You praise, honor, and all the glory. In Jesus' name, Amen.

For the husband raised in a different faith

ather, thank You for allowing me the privilege to pray, and thank You for my husband and the favor he has with You and with man. You have blessed him with health and overflowing abundance in finances. He has soundness of mind and you are continually drawing him near to Your heart. Thank You for the laborer who you will send to minister salvation to him. Bless the laborer's life with Your greatness. By faith I declare You have already saved my husband and filled him with Your sweet, precious gift of the

Holy Spirit and he has everlasting life. Thank You that You will baptize him in the Holy Spirit and he will live according to Your divine will.

Thank You that You will open the eyes of his understanding. Clear vision will be his. I pray he will accept Jesus as Lord and Savior and will not be deceived by false religions or doctrines. He will be intimately involved with Your Word and allow it to fill his soul daily. Lord, bless our marriage and give us Your wisdom. Teach my husband to lead our household. May he sit with our children and teach them Your Word and Your ways as he lives an exemplary life, one that our children will honor, admire, and follow after.

You have granted wisdom in his fatherhood and blessed us in health, strength, submission, and obedience. The children and I are a delight to him and bring him praise and no burdens. You have delivered him from worry, stress, and fear, and filled all voids in his life with your love, power, purpose, and divine direction.

Thank You for delighting him and delighting in him, I pray that You do something phenomenal for him. Do it, Father, in a way so he knows it was only You. Thank You for touching him and allowing him to experience You in a real and living way.

Father, Your Word instructs me to love my husband and, through my prayer, I manifest that love. You made me a wise woman. Therefore I build my house through prayer and thank You for helping me to maintain a strong foundation in You for my household. After You, my first concern is my husband and how I may please him. Thank You for creating

me and fearfully and wonderfully making my husband. In Jesus' name, Amen.

For the hard-working husband

*F*ather, I offer a prayer of thanksgiving to You for my husband and what You have done, continue to do, and will do in his life. You designed him to be a man of God, that everything my husband touches will prosper. You have given him the ability to gain wealth, and he uses that wealth to build our family and advance Your kingdom.

You have given him such wisdom and poured into him divine health and prosperity. My husband is a cheerful giver. He continuously brings our tithe to the storehouse, and increase abounds for him. The devourer is rebuked because of his diligent giving. My husband works hard to see a continual harvest.

You have given my husband a clean heart and, by Your Spirit, renewed a right spirit within him. Every day ungodly forces pull on my husband, but Your Word stands strong in his life and he does not compromise. He continues to live his life in a manner that is fully pleasing to You.

For the husband struggling with addiction

*F*ather, the Word of God says, *"If the Son makes you free, you shall be free indeed"* (John 8:36). My husband is addicted to alcohol/drugs, and I want him free from this addiction. Lord, You said, *"Whatever things you ask when you pray, believe that you receive them, and you will have them"* (Mark 11:24). I choose to believe, and therefore

I say that my husband will be free from this addiction and serve You, wholly and completely. Father, I know that You love my husband and want the best for him. Let Your love overwhelm him. Send a laborer across his path, someone to minister Your life to him. He does not belong to the world or to Satan. You paid a great price for his freedom. Let Your laborer reveal this to him. Open the eyes of his understanding so that he can see how the enemy is attempting to destroy his life.

I take authority over this addiction because the Word of God told me that I have victory and reign in this life, by Jesus Christ. With that authority, I confess my husband's liberty. I confess that he is home with me and that his life is committed to righteousness. I confess that his experience as a drug user will be a testimony for the nations of the delivering power of Jesus Christ. I confess that multitudes will see and know of the greatness of God and bring glory to You because of his testimony. Revelation 12:11 said that he would overcome *"by the blood of the Lamb and by the word of* [his] *testimony."* Thank You for the blood; thank You for this testimony.

I agree and line up with Your Word; I submit my emotions, fears, and pain to the authority of Your Word and Your love. I confess that my husband is free from this addiction. Greater is He that is in my husband than he that is in the world. I say, in all things, my husband is more than a conqueror. Thank You for Your love, thank You for Your Word, thank You for Your delivering power, thank You for the victory, thank You for all that will be done. In Jesus' name, Amen.

ABOUT THE AUTHOR

The ministry of Pamela M. Hines began in 1982, after her husband Darrell L. Hines was raised to life after being tragically struck by lightning.

Together, they pastor one of the most dynamic churches within the city of Milwaukee, and are the overseeing founders of several other Christian Faith Fellowship Churches. She is the cofounder of Dominion Fellowship, an outreach ministry encompassing a diversity of races and religious backgrounds that caters to the specific needs of husband-and-wife ministry teams.

Pamela has an anointing upon her life to minister to women. She is the founder of "The Women's Image Course," a powerful series of lessons designed to meet the needs of women. Her grace and message attracts women from a variety of racial, economical, and social backgrounds. Her aim is to empower women to be all that God has called them to be, focusing on the spirit, soul, and body. Pamela's earnest desire is to help the body of Christ walk in the knowledge and authority that God has given to them, and to strengthen its members through the ministry of God's Word.

Her message is practical and those who hear her will become challenged to be all that God desires them to be.

Resolving Conflict in Marriage
Darrell L. Hines

Are the wedding and honeymoon over? Have years passed since your marriage was filled with romance? Do you find yourselves divided as a couple for days, even weeks? If this is your story, now is the time to resolve the conflicts in your marriage. Darrell Hines calls on you to recognize the spiritual forces that are intent on destroying your marriage. Discover today how you can begin walking together in a new, stronger commitment! Learn how to build a relationship that faces difficulties, overcomes them, and emerges stronger than ever! This book is a must-read for all married couples and a powerful gift for those about to make wedding vows.

ISBN: 978-0-88368-729-1 • Trade • 224 pages

WHITAKER
HOUSE
www.whitakerhouse.com

Little Hickman Creek Series

by Sharlene MacLaren

Loving Liza Jane

Liza Jane Merriwether had come to Little Hickman Creek, Kentucky, to teach. She had a lot of love to give to her students. She just hadn't reckoned on the handsome stranger with two adorable little girls and a heart of gold that was big enough for one more.

Ben Broughton missed his wife, but he was doing the best he could to raise his two daughters alone. Still, he had to admit that he needed help, which is why he wrote to the Marriage Made in Heaven Agency for a mail-order bride. While he was waiting for a response, would he overlook the perfect wife that God had practically dropped in his lap?

ISBN: 978-0-88368-816-8 • Trade • 368 pages

Sarah, My Beloved

Sarah Woodward has come to Kentucky as a mail-order bride. But when she steps off the stage coach, the man who contacted her through the Marriage Made in Heaven Agency informs her that he has fallen in love with and wed another woman. With her usual stubborn determination, she refuses to leave until she finds out what God's reason is. Rocky Callahan's sister has died, leaving him with two young children to take care of. When he meets the fiery Sarah, he proposes the answer to both their problems—a marriage in name only. Can he let go of the pain in his past and trust God's plan for his life? Will she leave him or will they actually find a marriage made in heaven?

ISBN: 978-0-88368-425-2 • Trade • 368 pages

Courting Emma

Twenty-eight-year old Emma Browning has experienced a good deal of life in her young age. Proprietor of Emma's Boardinghouse, she is "mother" to an array of beefy, unkempt, often rowdy characters. Though many men would like to get to know the steely, hard-edged, yet surprisingly lovely proprietor, none has truly succeeded. That is, not until the town's new pastor, Jonathan Atkins, takes up residence in the boardinghouse.

ISBN: 978-1-60374-020-3 • **Available Spring 2008**

WHITAKER HOUSE

www.whitakerhouse.com